高等职业学校"十四五"规划跨境贸易专业群建设"岗课赛证"融通新形态精品教材

跨境电商英语

主　编：刘　文　赵秀丽　熊　莺
副主编：姚晓翠　陈淑媛

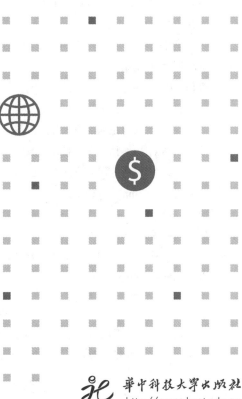

华中科技大学出版社
http://press.hust.edu.cn
中国·武汉

内 容 提 要

本书是高等职业学校跨境贸易专业群建设"岗课赛证"融通新形态系列教材之一。

全书内容以跨境电商运营专员岗位工作流程为主线,结合亚马逊电商平台,涵盖店铺注册、物流设置、产品标题和页面撰写、营销推广、退换货处理、客户评价处理等工作任务,旨在帮助学生学习、模仿并掌握亚马逊平台操作流程和语言表达技能。

本书可作为高等职业院校、高等专科院校、本科职业院校财经商贸类及语言类专业的教材。

图书在版编目(CIP)数据

跨境电商英语/刘文,赵秀丽,熊莺主编. —武汉:华中科技大学出版社,2023.6(2025.1重印)
ISBN 978-7-5680-9455-9

Ⅰ.①跨… Ⅱ.①刘… ②赵… ③熊… Ⅲ.①电子商务-英语-教材 Ⅳ.①F713.36

中国国家版本馆 CIP 数据核字(2023)第 109788 号

跨境电商英语　　　　　　　　　　　　　　　　　刘　文　赵秀丽　熊　莺　主编
Kuajing Dianshang Yingyu

策划编辑:周晓方　陈培斌　宋焱
责任编辑:刘　凯
封面设计:廖亚萍
责任校对:张汇娟
责任监印:周治超

出版发行:华中科技大学出版社(中国·武汉)　　　电话:(027)81321913
　　　　　武汉市东湖新技术开发区华工科技园　　　邮编:430223
录　　排:华中科技大学出版社美编室
印　　刷:武汉科源印刷设计有限公司
开　　本:787mm×1092mm　1/16
印　　张:15.5
字　　数:365 千字
版　　次:2025 年 1 月第 1 版第 2 次印刷
定　　价:58.00 元

本书若有印装质量问题,请向出版社营销中心调换
全国免费服务热线:400-6679-118　竭诚为您服务
版权所有　侵权必究

高等职业学校"十四五"规划跨境贸易专业群建设
"岗课赛证"融通新形态精品教材

主 编

刘 丹

副主编

吴金娇　　熊 莺

编 委

郭志颖　　梁川飞　　李肖爽

王姣蓉　　吴建霞　　严 丽

张凤秦

总 序
General Prologue

党的二十大报告强调,"推动货物贸易优化升级,创新服务贸易发展机制,发展数字贸易,加快建设贸易强国"。推动贸易强国建设是建设现代化经济体系的应有之义,也是全面建设社会主义现代化国家的必然要求,其中,数字贸易将赋予贸易强国建设新动能和新优势。大力发展数字贸易,发挥我国海量数据和超大规模市场优势,对于畅通经济循环,助力经济全球化发展,加快构建新发展格局,推动全球价值链变革,更好地满足人民群众的美好生活需要具有重要意义。

跨境电商正在成为数字服务经济新时代全球经济增长的新引擎。目前,中国在跨境电商市场规模、创新活跃度、数字化应用等衡量指标中居全球首位,具有很强的国际竞争力。然而,各层次跨境电子商务人才的缺乏,成为制约跨境电商及相关产业发展的瓶颈。探索跨境电商新职业标准制定、推动相应职业教育改革,培养适应时代、产业所需的高素质技术技能人才,有利于培育具有国际竞争力的跨境电商市场主体,构建优质跨境贸易生态和稳定全球跨境贸易供应链、产业链、价值链,推动经济结构调整、经济增长,以及带动更广范围的就业与拉动经济复苏。培养拥有国际视野与国际化能力、兼具数字技术知识和互联网思维,同时掌握国际商务运营与管理的复合型人才,将为跨境贸易产业的可持续发展提供长期动力,这不仅能够推动产业发展、提供社会就业、实现绿色可持续发展,更能够将中国主导的行业人才标准、中国教育教学体系推广至其他国家,从教育、文化、经济全方位推动人类命运共同体建设。

2021年4月中旬,中共中央政治局委员、国务院副总理孙春兰在全国职业教育大会上发表讲话时,首次提出职业教育"岗课赛证"综合育人。要求职业教育深化"三教"改革,"岗课赛证"综合育人,提高教育质量。2021年4月下旬,孙春兰在安徽调研时强调,要推动全国职业教育大会精神落地落实,要以"岗课赛证"引领"三教"改革。随后,教育部印发通知贯彻全国职业教育大会精神,要求加快完善人才培养体系,探索"岗课赛证"相互融合。2021年10月,中央办公厅、国务院办公厅印发《关于推动现代职业教育高质量发展的意见》,提出要完善"岗课赛证"综合育人机制,要求"按照生产实际和岗位需求设计开发课程,开发模块化、系统化的实训课程体系""深入实施职业技能等级证书制度""及时更新教学标准,将新技术、新工艺、新规范、典型生产案例及时纳入教学内容""把职业技能等级证书所体现的先进标准融入人才培养方案"等。这是较为系统地、权威地阐述了"岗课赛证"综合育人的核心要义。关于"岗课赛证"综合育人,我国具有良好的实施基础。职业技能比赛已经组织实施了十多年,2005年国务院提出"定期开展全国性的职业技能竞赛活动",2008年教育部提出"广泛开展职业院校技能竞赛活动,使技能竞赛成为促进教学改革的重要抓手和职业教育制度建设的一项重要内容"。2019年《国家职业教育改革实施方案》提出启动1+X证书制度试点工作以来,教育部、国家发改委、财政部、市场监管总局联合制定了《关于在院校实施"学历证书+若干职业技能等级证书"制度试点方案》,教育部办公厅、国家发改委办公厅、财政部办公厅印发了《关于推进1+X证书制度试点工作的指导意见》等系列文件,扎实推进1+X证书制度。在新时期,我国职业教育推进"岗课赛证"综合育人,需要进一步适应职业教育高质量发展的时代要求,适应经济社会发展的时代变化,不断迭代其内涵与实质、更替其路径与方法,紧扣"岗课赛证"综合育人的根本目标,将"岗课赛证"综合育人融入职业教育教学改革的各项举措。

为贯彻《国家职业教育改革实施方案》,推动专业升级和数字化改造,结合新专业目录的专业设置,落实立德树人的根本任务,建立"岗课赛证"融通综合育人的一体化新形态教材体系,华中科技大学出版社于2021年6月在武汉外语外事职业学院举办"岗课赛证"综合育人一体化教材编写研讨会。我院根据国家关于职业教育教材建设的相关落实文件,率先在省级高水平专业群——"多语种跨境贸易专业群"项目团队启动"岗课赛证"融通教材建设工作,推动教材配套资源和数字教材建设,高起点、高标准建设中国特色高质量职业教育教材体系。教材编写团队以学习者为中心出发,以职业能力成长为理念厘清逻辑关系,以对接岗位和工作过程为原则整合体系,以分层次、多场景的教学模式赋能课程实施,实现以"能力岗位匹配"客观需求到"岗位课程匹配"的主动供给。同时,多语种跨境贸易专业群教学团队优化教材建设机制,打造融合"岗""证""赛"的新型专业教材,教材内容及时体现产业生产技术发展动态,同时,将产业生产实践和技术升级的变化,及时反映在教材中。

职业教育作为类型教育,在人才培养、专业发展、课程开发、教材建设中有自身特点和规律,本系列教材融入和传承工匠精神,注重与工作岗位相适应,侧重劳动教育和生产实践。在编写理念上,注重弘扬工匠精神。教材开发中,注重将专业精神、职业精神、工匠精神、劳模精神等融入专业课程内容,整套教材的呈现遵循技术技能人才成长规律,遵循高职学生认知特点,突出理论与实践相统一。教材的编写逻辑以工作逻辑、学生认知为主要依据,以真实生产项目、工作任务、典型案例等形式组织教学单元,体现直观性、实用性、职业性等特征。利用"互联网+"技术,增加教材立体化开发,加快教材更新速度,适应新时代发展需要,从而提升教材建设在提高人才培养质量中的基础性作用,为推进职业教育高质量发展和现代职业教育体系建设改革、培养高素质技术技能型人才提供重要支撑。

武汉外语外事职业学院副院长

刘 丹

2023 年 6 月

前言
Preface

随着经济全球化、"互联网+"战略实施,以及大数据、云计算、区块链、智慧物流等技术的广泛应用,中国商贸业快速发展,作为推动经济一体化、贸易全球化的跨境电商新业态应运而生,持续发展壮大。党的二十大报告中,强调了加快建设贸易强国的重要性。跨境电商作为一种新的业态和模式,已经成为我国外贸发展的新动力、新途径和新机遇,对于外贸的转型升级和高质量发展也起到了积极的推动作用。从跨境电商出口目标市场来看,中国的跨境出口主要面向美国、英国、加拿大、澳大利亚等成熟的英语系国家。随着跨境电商的蓬勃发展和产业升级,规模化、精而细的行业特点使得该领域的人才需求越来越综合化,不仅需要这类人才具备国际贸易、电子商务、运营管理的专业知识和技能,还需要其有良好的外语水平和在线商务沟通能力,很多跨境电商企业在招聘人才时都提出了"跨境电商岗位职业技能+外语技能"的要求。为提高学生"互联网+"时代的涉外语言、商务和跨文化交际能力,结合商务英语、国际经济与贸易、跨境电子商务等专业的职业岗位能力要求,在充分调研和论证的基础上,我们策划和编写了《跨境电商英语》。该教材旨在通过标准规范的阅读材料、典型新颖的案例分析和实用多样的项目拓展,帮助学生了解并掌握未来工作岗位所需的跨境电商行业基础知识和岗位技能,提升学生的职场英语应用能力。

一、教材特色

(1)以实际工作任务为导向、以工作流程为主线,通过充分调研跨境电商业务各个岗位的主要工作,根据跨境电商平台各运营岗位典型工作任务,创造逼真的跨境电商英语学习情境。

(2)以亚马逊平台为基础,将英语学习融入工作任务,比如账户注册、产品上传、产品文案撰写、售前客服、发货操作、售后客服、客户营销等场景。

（3）通过多样化的实战练习强化语言的实际应用，将语言学习与跨境电商专业知识紧密联系起来。以英语能力培养为基础，以跨境电商职业技能培养为主线，以复合型应用能力为核心，帮助学生用英语熟练操作跨境电商平台。

二、教材结构

本教材共4个单元12个任务，围绕开店、产品上架、产品营销、客户服务等主题设置相应的工作任务。每个任务分为3个模块和1个"1+X"职业技能等级证书知识点讲解模块，具体如下：

模块1(Module One Warm-up)为导入，初步了解本单元主题。

模块2(Module Two Reading)为精读，通过语篇阅读学习行业英语词汇、短语、表达等，了解跨境电商专业知识。

模块3(Module Three Project Implementation)为实操，了解亚马逊平台中的英文词汇、表达等，熟悉平台操作。

"1+X"等级证书知识点模块(Notes for 1+X Certificate)为拓展阅读，旨在提升学生英语阅读能力和熟悉跨境电商"1+X"职业技能等级证书相关考点知识。

三、选择本书的理由

（1）词汇表达讲解详细，浅显易学。

（2）工作任务式编排，真实易懂。

（3）工作过程式设计，清晰明了。

（4）"1+X"证书考点结合，简单实用。

四、编写队伍

本教材由武汉外语外事职业学院刘文、赵秀丽、熊莺担任主编，姚晓翠、陈淑媛担任副主编。

本教材在编写的过程中得到"1+X跨境电子商务多平台运营职业技能等级证书"组织机构——厦门优优汇联有限公司的大力支持，在此对他们表示衷心的感谢！与此同时，我们得到了华中科技大学出版社领导、编辑等相关人员的鼎力支持，在此一并表示感谢！

由于时间紧迫、水平有限，错误与不妥之处在所难免，恳请广大读者不吝批评指正，以便修订时加以完善。

编　者

2023年1月

目录
Contents

Unit One Starting a Business on Amazon ………………………………… (1)

Task 1 Store Registration ………………………………………………… (2)

Task 2 Logistics …………………………………………………………… (17)

Task 3 Fulfillment by Amazon (FBA) …………………………………… (29)

Unit Two Creating a Product Listing ……………………………………… (45)

Task 4 Listing Products …………………………………………………… (46)

Task 5 Title Description …………………………………………………… (63)

Task 6 Product Description ……………………………………………… (75)

Unit Three Marketing ………………………………………………………… (89)

Task 7 Marketing Strategy ……………………………………………… (90)

Task 8 Amazon Advertising ……………………………………………… (105)

Task 9 Marketing outside Amazon Platform …………………………… (119)

Unit Four Customer Service ………………………………………………… (133)

Task 10 Customer Questions …………………………………………… (134)

Task 11 Returns ………………………………………………………… (148)

Task 12 Handling Negative Comments ………………………………… (163)

APPENDIX Ⅰ　Vocabulary　词汇表 ……………………………………………（179）

APPENDIX Ⅱ　Term　术语表 …………………………………………………（188）

课文参考译文 ……………………………………………………………………（192）

Unit One

Starting a Business on Amazon

Task 1 Store Registration

 Project Description

You are an employee of a cross-border company that intends to build an online store on Amazon. You need to have your store registration materials ready and register a store on Amazon.

 Project Requirement

· Complete registration on Amazon.

 Learning Goals

· Understand two types of account on Amazon.
· Master the store registration process.
· Master words and expressions related to store registration.

Module One　Warm-up

Look at the following pictures and discuss in pairs what you should prepare to start a business on Amazon?

A List of Things Needed to Start a Business on Amazon:

Module Two　Reading

Things You Must Know before Selling on Amazon

If you want to expand your company's selling reach, selling on Amazon (Fig. 1-1) is a straightforward process.

Since an Amazon business is a real business, there are a lot of things that you will need to consider and prepare for. Here are the documents and information you need to start your Amazon seller career. Make sure that you have them at hand before signing up for a seller account on Amazon:

(1) credit card information;
(2) bank account number;
(3) bank routing number;

Fig. 1-1　Amazon

(4) business license;

(5) phone number.

Amazon would ask you to provide additional documentation such as scanned copies of other documents like bank account statements, credit card statements, government-issued national ID, etc.

1-1　亚马逊平台介绍

To become an Amazon seller you must register yourself on Amazon Seller Central and make Amazon seller account. You need to choose the type of selling plan. Currently, there are two types of selling plans on Amazon: individual one and professional one (Fig. 1-2).

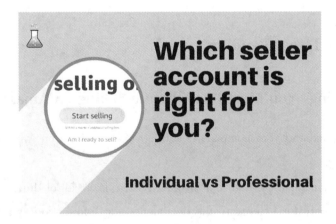

Fig. 1-2　Seller Account

Individual selling plan (individual account): There is no monthly fee of this account, although you can sell a maximum of 40 items a month and have access to 20 categories. There is a per-item fee of $0.99 that will be charged on every item sales. If you choose the individual account, you can keep your cost low. However, there are also many disadvantages. For example, you will not have the ability to advertise your products on Amazon.

Professional selling plan (professional account): There is a monthly subscription fee of $39.99 where you can sell more than 40 items monthly. A professional account holder has access to any categories. However, there are some restricted categories that can be accessed only after the approval. As a professional seller, you will receive a number of selling tools to help you run your business and manage inventory.

1-2 专业卖家计划的权益

Start by creating an account and filling out all of the necessary information. Add product listings (Fig. 1-3) and select whether you want to ship the products yourself or use Amazon's fulfillment service. Once everything is set up, you are ready to make your first sale!

Fig. 1-3 Listing on Amazon

New Words and Expressions

expand /ɪkˈspænd/ n. 发展(业务)
process /ˈprəʊses/ n. 过程; v. 处理
account /əˈkaʊnt/ n. 账户
documentation /ˌdɒkjʊmenˈteɪʃən/ n. 证明文件
scan /skæn/ n. 扫描
register /ˈredʒɪstə/ v. 注册
fee /fiː/ n. 费用
maximum /ˈmæksɪməm/ n. 最大量
item /ˈaɪtəm/ n. 商品; 项目
category /ˈkætɪɡərɪ/ n. 类目

subscription /səbˈskrɪpʃən/ *n.* 订阅,订购
restricted /rɪˈstrɪktɪd/ *adj.* 受限制的
approval /əˈpruːvəl/ *n.* 通过,批准
inventory /ˈɪnvəntərɪ/ *n.* 库存
at hand 在手边
sign up 注册
have access to 有(使用的)机会、权利
fill out 填写
set up 设置

Terms

bank account number   银行账号
bank routing number   银行识别码
bank account statement   银行对账单
credit card statement   信用卡对账单
government-issued national ID   政府发放的国民身份证
individual selling plan   个人销售计划
professional selling plan   专业销售计划
Amazon Seller Central   亚马逊卖家平台
business license   营业执照
product listing   产品刊登;产品页面
Amazon's fulfillment service   亚马逊物流服务

Exercises

Ⅰ. Write T for true or F for false in the brackets beside the following statements about the text.

1. You need to prepare documents and information before registering on Amazon.   (   )
2. A credit card is required to start your business on Amazon.   (   )
3. Phone number is not necessary information for Amazon seller to prepare.   (   )
4. There are two types of account on Amazon.   (   )
5. It is free to hold a professional account on Amazon.   (   )

6. There is no monthly fee for individual account.　　　　　　　　　（　）
7. A professional account holder can sell products of any categories.　（　）
8. Amazon sellers can sell a maximum of 40 items a month.　　　　（　）
9. Professional sellers will receive a number of selling tools to help them run their business and manage inventory.　　　　　　　　　　（　）
10. Amazon sellers can select whether they want to ship the products themselves or use Amazon's fulfillment service.　　　　　　　　（　）

II. Read the text again and fill in the blanks in the following sentences.

1. You need prepare _____ and _____ to start your business on Amazon, such as _____, _____, _____, _____, and phone number.
2. There are two types of account on Amazon: _____ and _____.
3. Additional documentation might also be required by Amazon, such as scanned copies of other documents like _____, _____, _____ national ID, etc.
4. There is no _____ of individual account, although you can sell a _____ of 40 items a month.
5. There is a monthly _____ of $39.99 where you can sell more than 40 items monthly.
6. A number of selling tools would be helpful for _____ sellers to _____ and _____.

III. Translate the following passage into Chinese.

There is a monthly subscription fee of $39.99 where you can sell more than 40 items monthly. A professional account holder has access to any categories. However, there are some restricted categories that can be accessed only after the approval. As a professional seller, you will receive a number of selling tools to help you run your business and manage inventory.

Module Three Project Implementation

A Step-by-step Guide on Setting up Your Amazon Seller Account

Once you have figured out what you plan on selling on Amazon, you will need to go through the Amazon seller registration process (Fig. 1-4).

Fig. 1-4　Amazon Registration

1. Visit *https://sell. amazon. com* to register on Amazon as a seller. Click on "Sign up" to create a new account (Fig. 1-5).

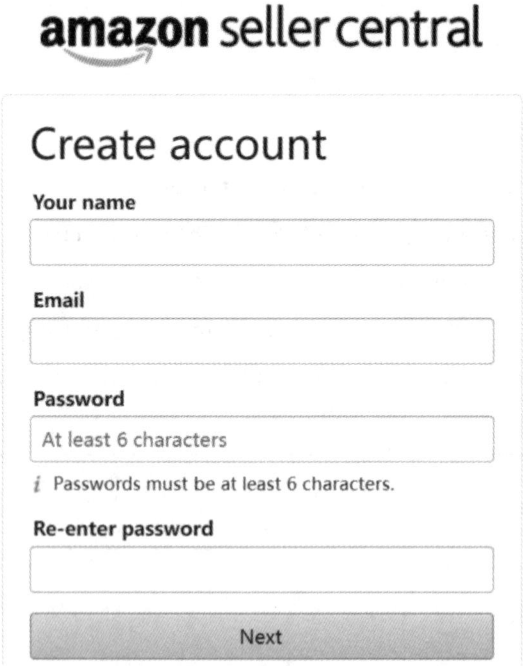

Fig. 1-5　Creating Account

2. Choose your "Business location" and "Business type" (Fig. 1-6).

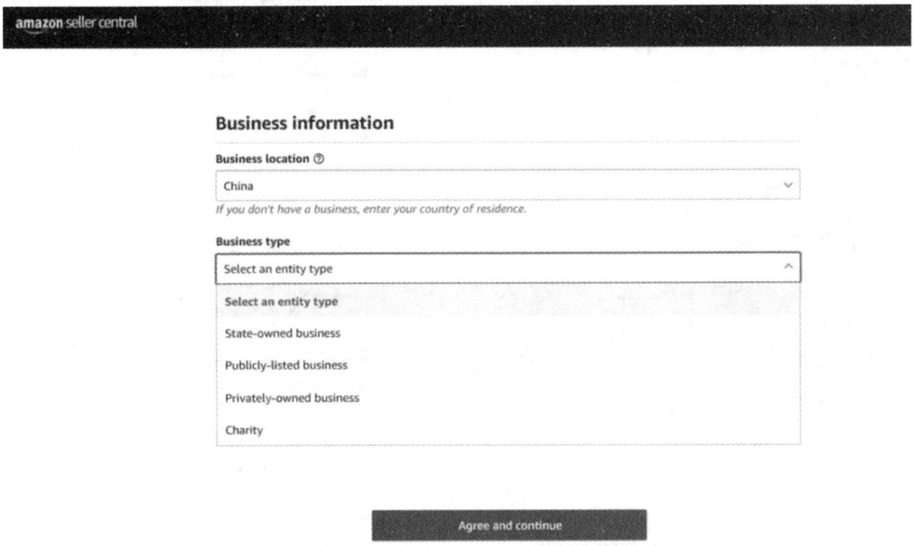

Fig. 1-6　Business Location and Type

Your business location refers to the country in which your business is located.

Your business type refers to your business entity from the following options.

(1) State-owned business;

(2) Publicly-owned business;

(3) Privately-owned business;

(4) Charity.

3. Complete a five-step wizard that collects your personal information (Fig. 1-7).

Step 1: Enter business information, such as your business name, company registration number, business address, zip code. Then give your phone number and verify it with PIN number through SMS or call.

Step 2: Enter seller information, such as your full name, country of citizenship, country of birth, date of birth, residential address, and phone number for verification.

Step 3: Enter your billing information (Fig. 1-8). First, verify banking information, including your bank account holder name, 9-digit routing number, bank account number and a valid credit card number. Second, you will need to enter your credit card details, including your credit card number, the date it expires on, card holder's name, and billing address.

1-3　亚马逊如何
转账付款

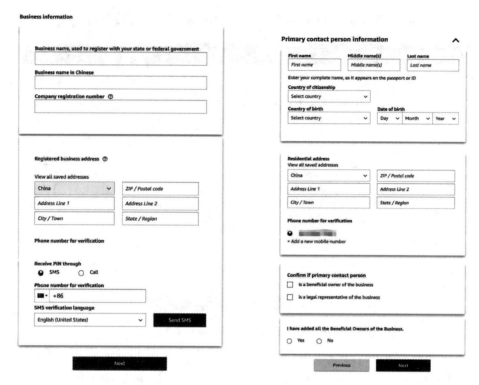

Fig. 1-7　Business and Seller Information

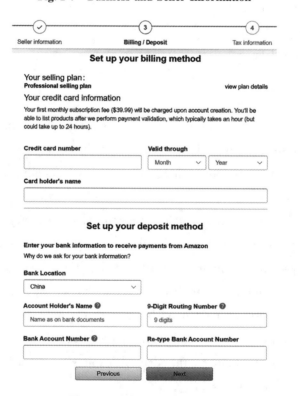

Fig. 1-8　Billing Information

Step 4: Add the information (Fig. 1-9) for your product(s) and Amazon store as follows.

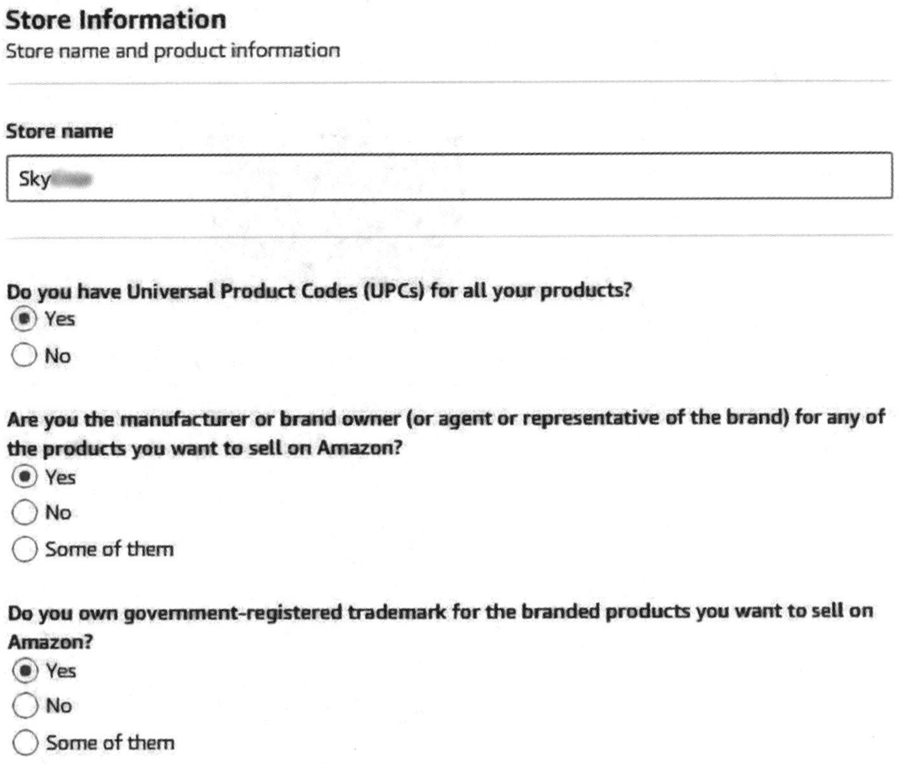

Store Information
Store name and product information

Store name
Sky____

Do you have Universal Product Codes (UPCs) for all your products?
◉ Yes
◯ No

Are you the manufacturer or brand owner (or agent or representative of the brand) for any of the products you want to sell on Amazon?
◉ Yes
◯ No
◯ Some of them

Do you own government-registered trademark for the branded products you want to sell on Amazon?
◉ Yes
◯ No
◯ Some of them

Fig. 1-9 Store Information

(1) The name of your Amazon store;

(2) Whether or not you have Universal Products Codes (UPCs) for your products;

(3) If you are the manufacturer and/or brand owner of the products you are selling;

(4) Whether you own a government-registered trademark for the branded products you want to sell on Amazon.

Step 5: Identity verification.

You will be asked to verify your identity by uploading images of your ID (license or passport) and business license (Fig. 1-10). When you have completed all of the other steps in the verification process, you will be asked to confirm the business address you provided previously. You will receive a postcard at that address, along with a verification code. When you receive the card, enter the code provided into the Enter code below field and click Next to finish the verification process. Once you are verified, you are in!

Fig. 1-10　Identity Verification

Exercises

I. Put the information in the right category.

1. bank account holder name
2. business address
3. residential address
4. manufacturer
5. date of birth
6. phone number
7. routing number
8. store name
9. country of citizenship
10. bank account number
11. image of ID

12. company registration number
13. credit card number
14. card holder's name
15. UPC
16. zip code
17. country of birth
18. brand owner
19. billing address
20. business name
21. government-registered trademark
22. postcard
23. image of business license
24. expiration date
25. verification code

A. Business information _____
B. Seller information _____
C. Billing information _____
D. Product and store information _____
E. Identity verification _____

Ⅱ. Finish the registration chart in English as required according to the company information provided below.

公司/企业名称	倍达科技有限公司
业务类型	私营企业
公司邮箱	Beidakeji@gmail.com
公司电话	18825601234
公司地址	武汉市东湖高新区高新二路16号
邮编	430073
公司注册号	432545256898512
店铺名称	Best Tech
法定代表人姓名	张三
法人身份信息(身份证号)	411115199512208562

续表

身份证有效期限	2018. 07. 11—2028. 07. 11
出生日期	1995. 12. 20
签发国	中国
永久住址	武汉市硚口区宝丰路100号
邮编	430030
收款账号(信用卡)	6222 0230 6110 7720 066
信用卡账单地址	武汉市硚口区宝丰路100号
邮编	430030
收款账号有效期至	2030年5月
持卡人姓名	张三
存款银行卡号	6222 0271 4817 9204 735
存款方式(9位数汇款路线)	121547154
品牌	Best
工厂员工数	500人
工厂地址	武汉市东湖高新区高新大道68号

Registration Chart

_____	business location	
	business type	
	business name	
	company registration number	
	business address	
	zip code	
	phone number	
_____	country of citizenship	
	country of birth	
	date of birth	
	residential address	
_____	bank account holder name	
	9-digit routing number	
	bank account number	
	credit card number	

continued Table

	credit card valid through	
	credit card holder's name	
	billing address	
	the name of your Amazon store	
	Do you have Universal Products Code (UPCs) for all your products?	
	Are you the manufacturer and/or brand owner for any of the products you want to sell on Amazon?	
	Do you own a government-registered trademark for the branded products you want to sell on Amazon?	

 Notes for 1+X Certificate

Selling Policies and Seller Code of Conduct

All sellers are expected to adhere to selling policies and seller code of conduct when listing products on Amazon. Seller offenses and prohibited content can result in suspension of Amazon account.

Sellers are required to act fairly and honestly on Amazon to ensure a safe buying and selling experience. All sellers must:

(1) Provide accurate information to Amazon and customers at all times;

(2) Not attempt to damage or abuse another seller, their listings or ratings;

(3) Not attempt to influence customers' ratings, feedback, and reviews;

(4) Not send unsolicited or inappropriate communications;

(5) Not contact customers except through Buyer-Seller Messaging;

(6) Not attempt to circumvent the Amazon sales process;

(7) Not operate more than one selling account on Amazon without a legitimate business need.

Examples of unfair activities include:

(1) Providing misleading or inappropriate information to Amazon or customers, such as by creating multiple detail pages for the same product or posting offensive product images;

(2) Manipulating sales rank (such as by accepting fake orders) or making claims about sales rank in product titles or descriptions;

(3) Attempting to increase the price of a product after an order is confirmed;

(4) Artificially inflating web traffic (using bots or paying for clicks, for example).

Sellers may not attempt to influence or inflate customers' ratings, feedback, and reviews. They may request feedback and reviews from their own customers in a neutral manner, but may not:

(1) Pay for or offer an incentive (such as coupons or free products) in exchange for providing or removing feedback or reviews;

(2) Ask customers to write only positive reviews or ask them to remove or change a review;

(3) Solicit reviews only from customers who had a positive experience;

(4) Review their own products or a competitor's products.

Violating the Code of Conduct or any other Amazon policies may result in actions against sellers' account, such as cancellation of listings, suspension or forfeiture of payments, and removal of selling privileges.

Task 2　Logistics

 Project Description

You have successfully registered an account on Amazon and opened a store. Before you start listing products for sale on Amazon, you need to configure your shipping settings to ensure they match what you want to offer to your customers.

 Project Requirement

· Configure shipping settings.

 Learning Goals

· Understand transportation modes of cross-border e-commerce logistics.
· Understand Amazon FBM.
· Master how to configure shipping settings.
· Master words and expressions related to logistics.

Module One   Warm-up

Read the passage and discuss with your partner the logistics modes in China and their characteristics.

Logistics refers to the overall process of managing how resources are acquired, stored, and transported to their final destination, including a wide variety of tasks and activities, such as managing how raw materials or inputs are acquired and transported to the business, how inventory and inputs are stored at the business' facilities, and how inventory is transported within the business and beyond. The term is used widely in the business sector, particularly by companies in the manufacturing sectors, to refer to how resources are handled and moved along the supply chain.

 Module Two   Reading

Cross-border E-commerce Logistics

Cross-border e-commerce logistics refers to cross-border e-commerce sellers transporting goods from their home countries to another country or region by land, air or sea. When doing cross-border e-commerce, it is very important to choose the right logistics modes (Fig. 2-1). Some platforms have high requirements for logistics, such as Amazon. These platforms designate logistics platforms for delivery, and have instructions on logistics timeliness.

The characteristics of cross-border e-commerce are small quantity, many batches, unstable orders and so on, so most of the merchants engaged in cross-border e-commerce adopt the following four logistics modes: traditional express service mode, special line mode, international express service mode, overseas storage mode.

1. Traditional Express Service Mode

The traditional express service is the postal service, which is the most important cross-border e-commerce logistics in China at present. One of its characteristics is wide coverage,

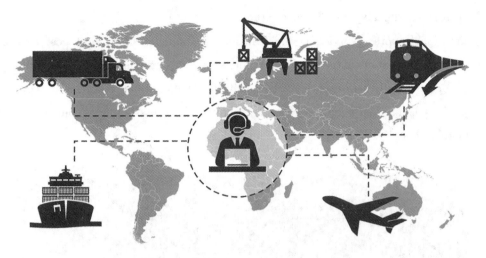

Fig. 2-1 Modes of Logistics in Cross-border E-commerce

covering more than 220 countries and regions around the world. It can deliver packages to almost every corner of the world. For instance, e-commerce ePacket (Fig. 2-2) from China Post is created specifically for online stores. It delivers small packages with low shipping rates because those packages are sent in bulk to reduce shipping costs. However, there are several requirements that need to be met.

Fig. 2-2 ePacket

These requirements have to do with the weight and dimensions of the product, along with the price of the product. For example, it can only send packages under 2 kilograms (about 4.4 lbs).

2. Special Line Mode

The special line generally sends the packages of many buyers in the same area to the destination country or region through the air line, and then distributes them through the local cooperative company or the logistics branch. The delivery time is faster than the postal service, and the price is lower than the commercial express. However, the scope of domestic cargo collection is limited, and sellers can only choose the line opened by the logistics company.

2-1 国际物流专线优缺点

3. International Express Service Mode

International express service is the fastest time-limited, the highest cost of transport (Fig. 2-3). Its biggest advantage is service and excellent customer experience, but because of its high cost, usually sellers do not choose the international express mode to send goods. So this mode accounts for a relatively small share in the cross-border e-commerce market. Sellers mainly choose DHL, TNT, FedEx and UPS.

Fig. 2-3　International Express Service

4. Overseas Warehouse Mode

The overseas warehouse mode is that the seller first prepares the goods in advance to the logistics warehouse of the destination country. After the customer orders in the seller e-commerce website or the third party store, the goods are shipped directly from the overseas warehouse to the customer. This can improve the timeliness of logistics to customers to bring quality logistics experience. But sellers usually choose only hot-selling items for overseas stock preparation (Fig. 2-4).

Fig. 2-4 Amazon Overseas Warehouse

New Words and Expressions

cross-border/ˈkrɒs bɔːdə(r)/ *adj.* 跨越国境的

e-commerce/iːˈkɒmɜːs/ *n.* 电子商务(同 e-business)

logistics/ləˈdʒɪstɪks/ *n.* 物流;组织工作;后勤

region/ˈriːdʒən/ *n.* 地区,区域,地方

mode/məʊd/ *n.* 方式;做法;方法

platform/ˈplætfɔːm/ *n.* 平台

designate/ˈdezɪgneɪt/ *v.* 指定;指派;选派;委任

timeliness/ˈtaɪmlɪnɪs/ *n.* 时间性;及时性

batch/bætʃ/ *n.* 一批;一组;一群

order/ˈɔːdə(r)/ *n.* 订单

merchant/ˈmɜːtʃənt/ *n.* 商人;批发商;(尤指)进出口批发商

adopt/əˈdɒpt/ *v.* 采用(……方法);采取(……态度)

express/ɪkˈspres/ *n.* 快件服务;快递服务;快运服务

centralized/ˈsentrəlaɪzd/ *adj.* 集中的;中央集权的

storage/ˈstɔːrɪdʒ/ *n.* 贮存,贮藏(空间)

coverage/ˈkʌvərɪdʒ/ *n.* 覆盖范围(或方式)

postal/ˈpəʊstl/ *n.* 邮寄的;邮政的;邮递的

rate/reɪt/ *n.* 价格;费用

dimension/dɪˈmenʃn/ *n.* 尺寸

destination/ˌdestɪˈneɪʃn/ n. 目的地；终点
distribute/dɪˈstrɪbjuːt/ v. 分发；分配；分送
commercial/kəˈmɜːʃl/ adj. 商业的；贸易的
cargo/ˈkɑːɡəʊ/ n. （船或飞机装载的）货物
share/ʃeə(r)/ n. （在多人参加的活动中所占的）一份；股份
warehouse/ˈweəhaʊs/ n. 仓库；货栈；货仓
account for （数量或比例上）占
in advance 提前；事先，预先

Terms

China Post　中国邮政
ePacket　e邮宝
special line　专线
commercial express　商业快递
overseas warehouse　海外仓库

Exercises

Ⅰ. Write T for true or F for false in the brackets beside the following statements about the text.

1. Not all platforms have high requirements for logistics.　　　　（　　）
2. The features of cross-border e-commerce are small quantity, many batches, and so on.　　　　（　　）
3. International express mode is the most important logistics mode of cross-border e-commerce logistics in China.　　　　（　　）
4. There is no weight restriction for the package using China Post.　　　　（　　）
5. Special line is to transport goods of sellers in the same area to the destination country.　　　　（　　）
6. The special line service is faster than the traditional express service.　　　　（　　）
7. International express service is the most expensive compared to other delivery services.　　　　（　　）
8. Sellers prefer to use international express service to deliver their goods because it offers fast delivery.　　　　（　　）

9. Sellers have to deliver their goods in advance to the warehouse of the destination country. ( )
10. Sellers often prepare all their goods to the overseas warehouse in advance. ( )

II. Read the text again and fill in the blanks in the following sentences.

1. Cross-border e-commerce sellers _____ goods from their home countries to another country or _____ by land, air or sea.
2. There are four logistics modes _____ by most of the merchants who _____ cross-border e-commerce.
3. The postal service _____ more than 220 countries and regions around the world.
4. ePacket from China Post is created specifically for _____, offering low shipping _____ as it delivers the small packages _____ to _____ shipping cost.
5. The package sent via special line is transported through the _____ before it is _____ through the local cooperative company or the _____.
6. The international express service mode _____ a relatively small _____ in the cross-border _____ market.
7. The goods from the overseas warehouse are shipped directly to the customer _____ the customer places an order online, _____ can improve the _____ of logistics to customers to bring _____ logistics experience.

III. Translate the following passage into Chinese.

E-commerce ePacket from China Post is created specifically for online stores. It delivers small packages with the lowest shipping rate because those packages are sent in bulk to reduce shipping costs. However, there are several requirements that need to be met. These requirements have to do with the weight and dimensions of the product, along with the price of the product. For example, it can only send packages under 2 kilograms (4.4 lbs).

Module Three Project Implementation

A Guide to Shipping Settings for Amazon FBM

Fulfillment by Merchant (FBM) is a method of selling on Amazon in which sellers list their products on Amazon, but handling the storage and all aspects of order fulfillment themselves (or through another third-party). If you use FBM to start your business on Amazon, be sure that your shipping settings match what you want to offer to your customers.

To configure shipping settings, go to Settings (Fig. 2-5) in the upper-right corner of Seller Central, click Shipping Settings. The Shipping Settings page appears.

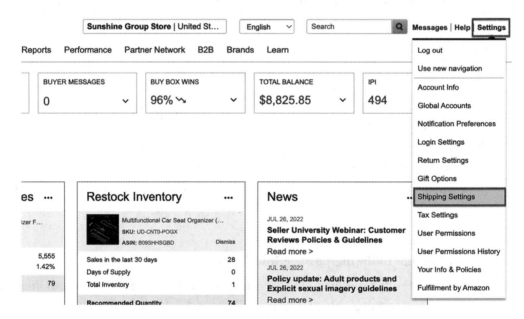

Fig. 2-5 Shipping Settings Access

Check the default shipping address at the top in the General shipping settings (Fig. 2-6). If you are shipping from a different location, press the Edit button, enter the location's name and address, and press Save.

Go to Shipping Templates tab (Fig. 2-7). There is a Migrated Template, which is set as your default template unless you change the default to a different one. Click Create a new shipping template. Give a name to the template as there may be different templates according to the needs in the future, which is convenient for quick selection.

Fig. 2-6　General Shipping Settings

Fig. 2-7　Shipping Templates

Amazon offers two methods for calculating shipping rates that you charge to your customers in Rate Model. You can choose either Per Item/Weight-Based or Price Banded. Per Item/Weight-Based will calculate the shipping price per item or per pound (lb), plus a fixed fee. Price Banded will calculate the shipping cost based on the shopper order price. You can customize different "bands", such as charging $2 shipping for orders between $1 and $10, $4 shipping for orders between $10 and $20, and so on.

Since your shipping costs are usually based on size and weight, it usually makes sense to go with the Per Item / Weight-Based option.

Choose delivery options. You have several choices on what delivery options you will offer. You start with choosing one or more of these options:

(1) Standard Shipping;

(2) Expedited Shipping;

(3) Two-Day Delivery;

(4) One-Day Delivery;

(5) Same-day Delivery;

(6) International Shipping.

Select regions where you will deliver. To change your region settings (Fig. 2-8), click Edit. If you sell in the US, Amazon will let you select/deselect Alaska, Hawaii, and all US protectorates (territories that are not US states).

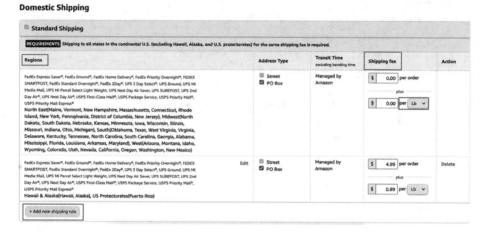

Fig. 2-8 Regions and Shipping Rates

Set your shipping rates in each delivery options. You can include a flat rate per order charge plus a fee per item or per pound. Click on the drop-down arrow to switch between charging by item or by pound. Your options here are customizable.

Now, You have completed creating your shipping template!

2-2 FBM 发货流程

Exercises

I. Translate the following words or terms into English.

1. 配送设置_____
2. 卖家平台_____
3. 右上角_____
4. 默认配送地址_____
5. 配送模板选项卡_____
6. 运费_____
7. 订单价格_____
8. 运输成本_____
9. 统一费率_____
10. 下拉箭头_____

II. Answer the following questions.

1. What does the seller need to do with FBM method?

___

2. What are the methods offered by Amazon to calculate shipping rate?

___

3. Why is the Price Banded option is not recommended in the text?

___

4. What are the delivery options provided by Amazon?

___

III. Complete the flow chart.

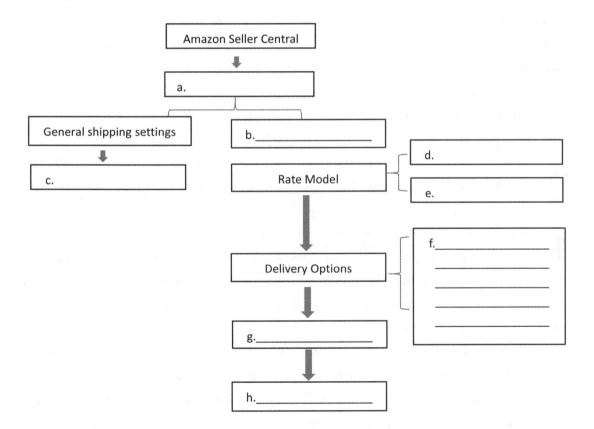

Notes for 1+X Certificate

Understanding Amazon FBM

Why should a seller consider Amazon FBM? Is it a viable option for your Amazon business? Compared with other fulfillment methods, FBM offers many advantages over other fulfillment. The benefits of FBM are as follows.

(1) No additional Amazon fees. FBM has the main advantage of saving money on referral fees and order fulfillment costs. You also do not have to worry about paying Amazon any storage fees.

(2) Control over packaging and shipping. When using FBM, you can control how your products are packaged and shipped. Your customer's first impression of your product is created by your packaging, and this impression is a lasting one. Eye-catching packaging will make your shop really stand out. You also can use different shipping methods, such as priority or overnight shipping, to get your products to customers as quickly as possible.

FBM can be a good option for many, but it is not without drawbacks. Here is a list of some of the biggest downsides of being an FBM seller.

(1) More responsibility. An FBM store means that you will have a greater list of responsibilities and duties to attend to. Not only are you responsible for sourcing and acquiring inventory, but you are also responsible for order processing and shipping. Shipping from China means a longer total delivery time, more complicated logistics, and less direct influence over product quality. Sellers may grow weary of fielding questions and dealing with issues relating to subsequent returns and exchanges. This is made even more stressful by Amazon's emphasis on customer satisfaction: If there are issues with the order, you may face penalties on your seller account.

(2) Extra overhead fees. Although you will not have to pay Amazon for shipping, storage, and fulfillment, you will still have to pay your own fulfillment and shipping fees. If you have to rent a space to store your inventory, you will have to pay for that as well. What's more, if your operation grows past a certain point, you may even have to hire employees or a third-party company for additional help.

Task 3 Fulfillment by Amazon (FBA)

 Project Description

To further boost sales and enhance customer experience, your company decides to use the Amazon FBA service. You need to create an FBA shipping plan before sending your products to Amazon's warehouse.

 Project Requirement

· Create an FBA shipping plan.

 Learning Goals

· Understand Amazon FBA.
· Master how to create an FBA shipping plan.
· Master words and expressions related to FBA shipping plan.

Module One   Warm-up

The Chart below shows the factors that influence online purchase decisions in the United States and the United Kingdom in 2022. Discuss with your partners based on your own experience.

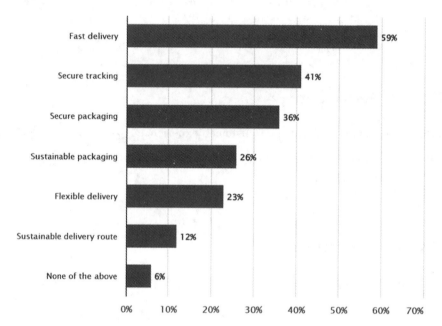

Factors Influencing Online Purchase Decisions in US and UK (2022)

 ## Module Two   Reading

Amazon FBA

When selling products through Amazon, apart from Fulfillment by Merchant (FBM), there is another method that the majority of Amazon sellers use: Fulfillment by Amazon (FBA) (Fig. 3-1). FBA is a method in which a seller (or a seller's supplier) sends products directly to Amazon's warehouses (Fig. 3-2). Amazon then manages all storage, packs the products and ships them directly to the customer. It also handles customer service and returns.

FBA could be the most beneficial option for some sellers. Amazon's FBA program has a whole host of benefits that will come in handy for inexperienced sellers using this platform.

Fig. 3-1 How Amazon FBA Works

Fig. 3-2 Amazon's Warehouses

Hands-off order fulfillment. Sellers will be responsible for sourcing and acquiring inventory, preparing orders, and sending them to Amazon to be processed. That is where their responsibilities end. They can focus on other areas of their business and can give more attention to growing their company.

3-1 黄金购物车

Avoid dealing with customer service issues. Amazon takes care of any customer service issues. For many online retailers, customer service represents a huge amount of time, money, and resources.

Eligibility for Prime delivery. If you pay close attention to listings, you will notice that sellers with Prime delivery often control the Buy Box (a yellow button). This is because Amazon prefers sellers who can guarantee quick delivery and with Amazon FBA, sellers are eligible for Prime delivery (Fig. 3-3).

It is important to note that more than 80% of all sales on Amazon are directly from sellers who control the yellow button. It provides a massive boost to sales.

Fig. 3-3 Amazon Prime Shipping

Avoid dealing with returns. Sellers will not have to handle any customer returns—Amazon takes care of that for them. Dealing with returns takes up a lot of time and energy.

While FBA comes with some impressive benefits, it does have some drawbacks, too.

Extra fees. Unfortunately, Amazon does not offer these services for free. Additional fees will have to be paid each month (Fig. 3-4). These fees include a monthly subscription fee, referral fees, storage fees, and fulfillment fees. Fees vary depending on the size, weight, and type of product being shipped.

Fees for Referring a Customer

Picking & Packing and Shipping Fees

Storage Fee

Fig. 3-4 FBA Fees

Increased returns. Many FBA merchants notice a greater amount of returns under the FBA program than the FBM program (Fig. 3-5). Amazon has a no-questions-asked returns policy. While this is great news for customers, it does result in more orders being returned.

Long-term inventory costs. Amazon charges for storage. If any of inventories are left lying in the warehouses or order fulfillment centers for a long time, extra fees will be charged. The cost of this varies depending on the amount of space the inventory takes up, as well as how long it has been in storage.

Fig. 3-5　Holiday Returns

New Words and Expressions

majority /məˈdʒɒrəti/ n. 大部分;大多数
supplier /səˈplaɪə(r)/ n. 供应者;供应商;供货方
pack /pæk/ v. 将……打包;把……装箱
return /rɪˈtɜːn/ n. 退货
option /ˈɒpʃn/ n. 可选择的事物;选择
hands-off /ˌhændz ˈɒf/ adj. 不介入的;放手的
source /sɔːs/ v. 寻找(产品或原料的)货源
issue /ˈɪʃuː/ n. 问题
retailer /ˈriːteɪlə(r)/ n. 零售商;零售店
resource /rɪˈsɔːs/ n. 资源;物力;财力
eligibility /ˌelɪdʒəˈbɪlɪti/ n. 有资格;具备条件;合适
boost /buːst/ v. 使增长;使兴旺
drawback /ˈdrɔːbæk/ n. 缺点;不利条件
vary /ˈveəri/ v. (根据情况)变化,变更,改变
a (whole) host of 大量的
come in handy 有用处
take up 占用,花费(时间、空间或精力)

Terms

Fulfillment by Merchant（FBM）　亚马逊卖家自配送
Fulfillment by Amazon（FBA）　亚马逊物流
subscription fee　订阅费
storage fee　库存仓储费
fulfillment fee　执行费

Exercises

Ⅰ. Write T for true or F for false in the brackets beside the following statements about the text.

1. There are two types of seller fulfillment methods on Amazon, Fulfillment by Merchant and Fulfillment by Amazon.　　（　　）
2. With Fulfillment by Merchant, products sold on Amazon are shipped to customers by Amazon.　　（　　）
3. It is the sellers who are responsible for storage, packing and shipping to customers with Fulfillment by Amazon.　　（　　）
4. Sellers on Amazon have to send their products to Amazon's warehouses.　（　　）
5. Amazon FBA can save time and help sellers grow their business.　（　　）
6. Customer service may consume a lot of time for many online retailers.　（　　）
7. Fast delivery services can drive sales on Amazon.　（　　）
8. Amazon would only charge the sellers for storage with Fulfillment by Amazon.　　（　　）
9. It is noticed that there are less returns under the FBM program than the FBA program.　　（　　）
10. You would pay more money if you leave your inventory in Amazon warehouses for a long time.　　（　　）

Ⅱ. Read the text again and fill in the blanks in the following sentences.

1. In addition to dealing with customer service and _____, Amazon is responsible for _____, _____ and ships them directly to the customer.

2. _____ has lots of _____ that will be useful for _____ merchants on Amazon.
3. Before sending products to Amazon, sellers need to _____ and _____ inventory, and _____.
4. Merchants with FBA have to pay _____, _____, _____, and _____.
5. The cost of long-term inventory is different in _____ and _____.

III. Translate the following passage into Chinese.

Sellers will be responsible for sourcing and acquiring inventory, preparing orders, and sending them to Amazon to be processed. That is where their responsibilities end. They can focus on other areas of their business and can give more attention to growing their company.

Module Three Project Implementation

How to Create an Amazon FBA Shipping Plan

If you want to sell products with Amazon FBA, you will need to ship them into an FBA warehouse so Amazon can fulfill your orders for you. To do that you must know how to create a shipping plan on Amazon. Only by understanding the specific Amazon FBA delivery process can we successfully deliver the product to Amazon. This article will break down the "Send to Amazon" process step-by-step.

1. Choose inventory to send

Log in to Amazon Seller Central, click Manage All Inventory in the Inventory tab to enter the inventory management interface. Sellers can find products by searching for SKU, title, and ASIN on the inventory management page.

3-2 SKU、ASIN

Select the product to be converted, click the drop-down next to the edit menu and choose Change to Fulfilled by Amazon (Fig. 3-6).

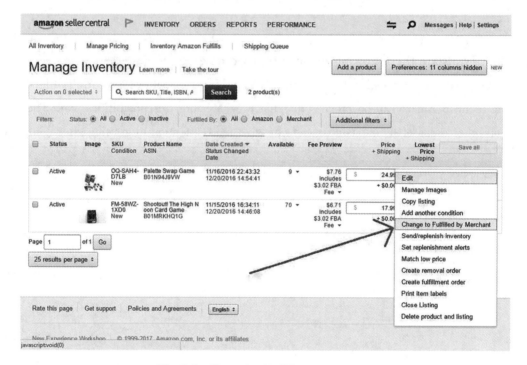

Fig. 3-6　Change to Fulfilled by Amazon

1) Shipping address and destination marketplace

Select a "Ship from address" and "Marketplace destination" so that Amazon knows where the goods are coming from and to which they will be sent (Fig. 3-7).

Fig. 3-7　Shipping Address and Destination Marketplace

2) Packing details

Amazon requires that you enter the packing details for each of the boxes you are sending to FBA warehouses (Fig. 3-8). There are two types of packing: "Individual units" and "Case-packed units". The "Individual units" option should be selected when sending packages containing one or more products of varying quantities and conditions. The "Case-packed Products" option should be selected when shipping products that have the same SKU. In this case, each shipment contains the same number of products.

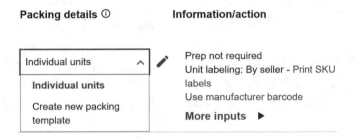

Fig. 3-8   Packing Details

If you choose the "Individual units" option, select the correct prep category (usually "No prep needed").

When sending case-packed units for the first time you will need to create a new packing template (Fig. 3-9). Here you can enter the dimensions, weight and number of units per carton you will be sending in.

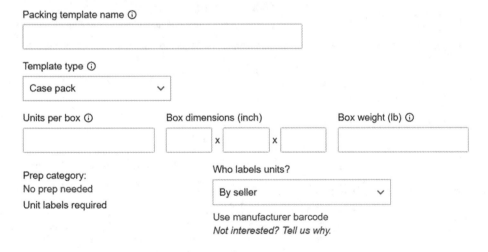

Fig. 3-9   Packing Template

3) Product label

Every product sent to Amazon's FBA warehouse must be labelled. There is a fee to have Amazon label them. If you choose to label by yourself, select "By seller" under "who labels units", and select the label paper of the corresponding specification to print the label (Fig. 3-10).

Fig. 3-10   Product Labels Stickers

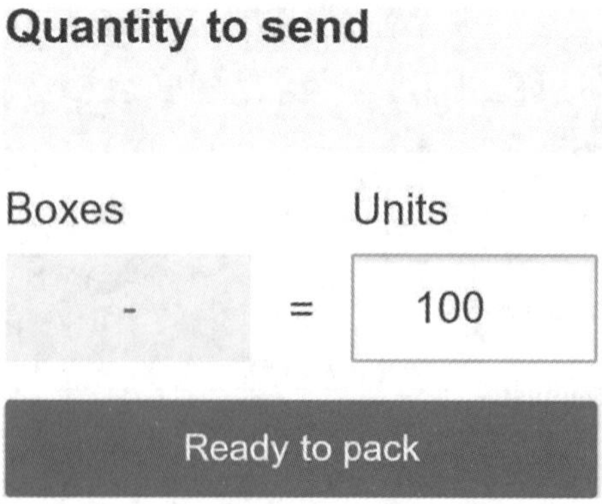

4) Quantities

Once you have entered all the packing details for each product in your FBA shipment, enter the number of boxes you are sending for each SKU and click the "Ready to pack" button (Fig. 3-11).

Fig. 3-11   Quantities

2. Confirm shipping

Review your shipment, set the ship date, the shipping mode, and the shipping carrier (Fig. 3-12). You need to select the shipping mode (Small parcel delivery and Less than truckload) and shipping carrier (Amazon-partnered carrier and Non-partnered carrier). Small parcel delivery (SPD) involves goods arriving at Amazon in individual cartons. This is the best for small shipments. Less than truckload (LTL) involves multiple cartons being packed onto pallets which is the shipping method recommended for larger shipments.

Fig. 3-12 Ship Date & Shipping Mode

You can select either "Amazon-partnered carrier" or "Non-Amazon-partnered carrier" as your shipping carrier (Fig. 3-13). Here you can see which warehouse Amazon has assigned products to.

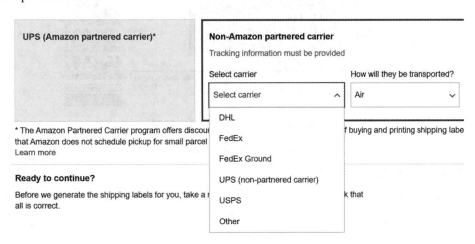

Fig. 3-13 Shipping Carriers

3. Print box labels

Print the box label, sticking it to the outer box after packing (Fig. 3-14, Fig. 3-15).

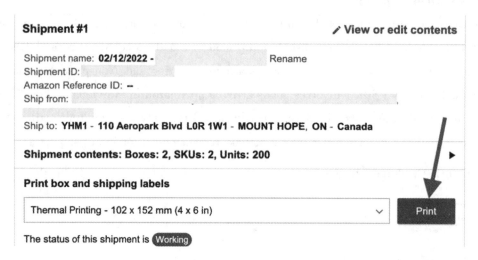

Fig. 3-14　Print Box Labels

Fig. 3-15　A Box Label

4. Tracking details

If you have chosen to use a non-Amazon-partnered carrier, fill in the tracking number, mark the order as shipped.

Exercises

I. Translate the following terms into English.

1. 库存选项卡 _____
2. 管理界面 _____
3. 库存量单位 _____
4. 亚马逊标准识别码 _____
5. 目标商城 _____
6. 装箱模板 _____
7. 包装类型 _____
8. 配送方式 _____
9. 配送商 _____
10. 运单号 _____

II. Answer the following questions.

1. How to find your products in Amazon Seller Central?

   _____

2. If you are to send different products to Amazon FBA, which type of packing do you choose? Why?

   _____

3. What is the information required in a FBA packing template?

   _____

4. Which shipping mode is the best choice for large shipments? Why?

   _____

III. Draw a flow chart by yourself according to the text and present it orally.

Notes for 1+X Certificate

Amazon FBA Packaging Requirements

Amazon FBA has specific requirements for how you package products to ensure that they can sell them. Here is a comprehensive list of Amazon FBA packaging requirements.

(1) All items must be wrapped individually.

(2) There must be two inches of cushioning between each item and the interior of the box.

(3) All products must be packaged in a secure, six-sided box. Flaps must be functional & intact.

(4) If you are using pallets, each pallet must be labeled four times. Labels should be placed on the center of each side.

(5) All boxes on a pallet must also be labeled individually.

(6) Each box must include its own FBA shipment label. These can be found in the—Shipping Queue on Seller Central.

(7) If using a master carton, you will need to place your unique shipping label on the master carton.

(8) You may reuse boxes—but they must be rigid and free from old shipping labels or markings.

(9) Use a single address label clearly marked with the proper delivery and return information. Amazon must have a return address in order to properly manage your inventory, in case they must send it back.

(10) Choose boxes that are under 25" on any given side and under 50 lb in weight.

(11) Use approved packing materials, like polyethylene foam sheeting, bubble wrap, air pillows, and sheets of paper. Do not use packing peanuts, foam strips, crinkle wrap, styrofoam, or shredded paper.

Each individual unit must be labeled properly according to the below labeling standards.

(1) Products must be packaged in accordance with the category in which they are sold.

(2) If you are selling a multi-pack, these must be clearly labeled as such.

(3) Products over 10 pounds, products that fail a 3-foot drop test, or particularly vulnerable products may require overboxing to secure the package.

(4) When packaging in cases, each case must contain the same number of identical products with the same SKU. You may include up to 150 items per case maximum.

(5) Expiration dates must be labeled clearly in MM-DD-YYYY format when applicable.

 Supplementary Reading

3-3 丝绸之路电子商务促进
"一带一路"国家间贸易

Unit Two

Creating a Product Listing

Task 4　Listing Products

 Project Description

In order to drive sales and achieve success on Amazon, as an operations specialist, you will need to create a product listing.

 Project Requirement

· Complete a product listing on Amazon.

 Learning Goals

· Understand the meaning, importance and components of Amazon product listings.

· Master the process of creating a product listing, and correctly fill in the product information.

· Master words and expressions related to product listings.

Module One　Warm-up

Look at the following picture and discuss in pairs what information you should prepare to list on Amazon?

 Module Two　Reading

Product Listing

Product listing (Fig. 4-1) is the process of uploading products and services to an e-commerce site, and completing with all the important details. It can also be classified as a data entry job to enter your company's products and services under the proper categories whether your e-commerce store is on Amazon, eBay, Magento, or any other platform. Products listed on e-commerce sites are filtered by customers according to color, size, shape, price, and so on. Proper product listing ensures that your products are properly classified so that they show up when someone searches for them.

4-1　主流跨境电商平台

Every element on the product page must be carefully thought out with the goal to offer the best shopping experience to customers. The process of product listing would also involve

Fig. 4-1 Product Listing

choosing the best photos to represent your product, highlighting your bestsellers and new offers, and ensuring that users can seamlessly navigate through your online store.

Product listing pages can usually be the first place your online store visitors land in when they search for products using search engines (Fig. 4-2). A solid product listing page has a direct impact on buyer perception, user experience, and sales. Think of it as you are making a first impression to your customers. Of course, you want to look professional, organized, and welcoming. The way you present your products is definitely an important part of running an e-commerce business (Fig. 4-3).

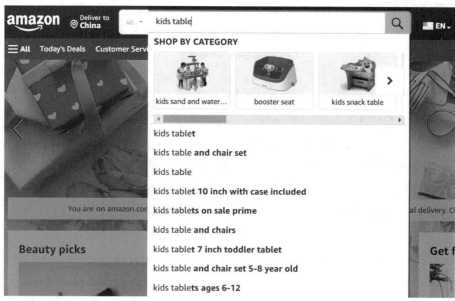

Fig. 4-2 Amazon Search Engine

Unit Two　Creating a Product Listing

Fig. 4-3　Product Listing Images

A good product listing page can boost your conversion rates (Fig. 4-4). You may already be implementing solid marketing campaigns, all leading interested customers to your store. You must ensure then that your product listing page serves its purpose well to make shopping in your store a good experience for every customer. They will check your products out and you can be sure they will be more inclined to make a purchase if you have well-crafted product descriptions, attractive images, easy navigation, and complete information on your product listing page.

4-2　转化率

Fig. 4-4　Conversion Rates

Amazon sells over 353 million different items, resulting in near-endless competition in the Amazon marketplace. Even if you have a high-quality product to sell, you will not be able to sell it if customers can not locate it among a sea of competitors. Therefore, you'd better optimize these listings (Fig. 4-5) so that shoppers will be able to search for and find those products with ease!

Fig. 4-5　Making More Sales

New Words and Expressions

upload /ˌʌpˈləʊd/ v. 上传
detail /ˈdiːteɪl/ n. 详情；细节
classify /ˈklæsɪfaɪ/ v. 将……分类
filter /ˈfɪltə(r)/ v. 筛选；过滤
layout /ˈleɪaʊt/ n. 布局
represent /ˌreprɪˈzent/ v. 代表
bestseller /ˌbestˈselə/ n. 畅销品
seamless /ˈsiːmləs/ n. 无缝的
navigate /ˈnævɪɡeɪt/ v. (网站) 导航
perception /pəˈsepʃn/ n. 看法；见解
conversion /kənˈvɜːʃn/ n. 转换；转化
implement /ˈɪmplɪmənt/ n. 贯彻；执行
incline /ɪnˈklaɪn/ v. (使) 倾向于
have a keen eye for detail 善于观察细节
search engine 搜索引擎

Terms

conversion rate 转化率

product description 产品描述

Exercises

Ⅰ. **Write T for true or F for false in the brackets beside the following statements about the text.**

1. Product listing is the process of uploading products and services to Amazon only. (　　)
2. Customers usually choose products they want according to color, size, shape, price, and so on. (　　)
3. Proper product listing can help to show your products to customers. (　　)
4. The listing page must be designed for offering the best shopping experience to customers. (　　)
5. Product listing pages can usually be the first place your online store visitors land in when they search for products. (　　)
6. The sales depend on the quality of products only. (　　)
7. The way you present your products is definitely an important part of running an offline shop. (　　)
8. Your conversion rates can be improved by a good product listing page. (　　)
9. If you want customers to make a purchase in your store, you must ensure that your listing page can offer more discount. (　　)
10. Product descriptions, attractive images, and easy navigation are important parts for a product listing page. (　　)

Ⅱ. **Read the text again and fill in the blanks in the following sentences.**

1. When you _____ your products and services with all the important _____ on an e-commerce site, the process is called as _____.
2. Product listing can also be classified as a data entry job to enter your company's _____ under the proper categories on any e-commerce platform.

3. Choosing _____ to represent your product, and highlighting your _____ and new offers are included in the process of product listing.

4. A good product listing page can boost your _____ .

5. In order to enable customers to locate your products among a sea of competitors, you'd better _____ product listings so that shoppers will be able to _____ and find those products with ease!

Ⅲ. Translate the following passage into Chinese.

Every element on the product page must be carefully thought out with the goal to offer the best shopping experience to customers. The process of product listing would also involve choosing the best photos to represent your product, highlighting your bestsellers and new offers, and ensuring that users can seamlessly navigate through your online store.

Module Three Project Implementation

Creating an Amazon Listing

The process to create a single listing on Amazon is a rather simple and an intuitive one; it is just a matter of knowing where to go to get started and what fields to fill out. When signed into your Amazon Seller Central, travel to "Catalog">"Add Products" (Fig. 4-6).

On this page, enter your product name, UPC, EAN, or ISBN to search. If Amazon does not find an existing listing related to your query, you can then click "Create a new listing" to start the creation process (Fig. 4-7).

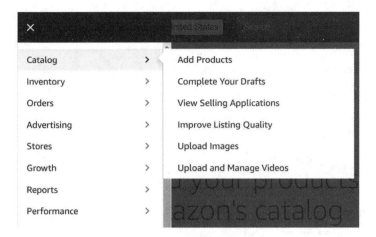

Fig. 4-6　Add Products

Fig. 4-7　Find Your Products

The first thing you must determine is the "Category" your product fits into. You can either utilize the search feature to help you narrow down categories, or you can manually click through the product categories to drill down to an appropriate sub-category (Fig. 4-8). Once you find your category, click on that hyperlink to bring you to your listing creation page. This page will display multiple tabs grouping together similar listing fields together, and this is where our content creation process begins.

4-3　UPC, EAN, ISBN

Vital Info

You will need to fill out the Product ID with UPC, EAN, or ISBN, the product name with your optimized title, your manufacturer, and your brand name (Fig. 4-9). Often times, manufacturer and brand name are the same, but please note that the brand name is what displays just below the title on a product detail page. It is very important the spelling is correct in these two fields from the beginning, as it is one of the harder fields to update post-creation. If you are ever unsure what to input into a field, Amazon provides small information icons next to the fields that can help guide you in the right direction.

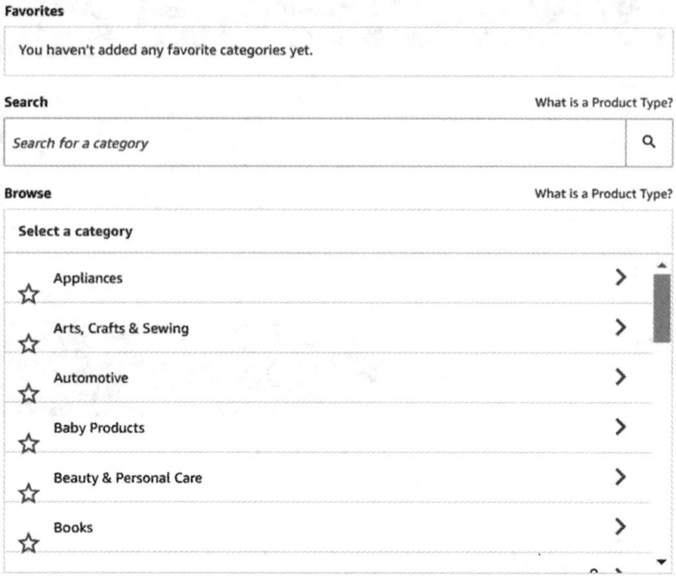

Fig. 4-8　Category

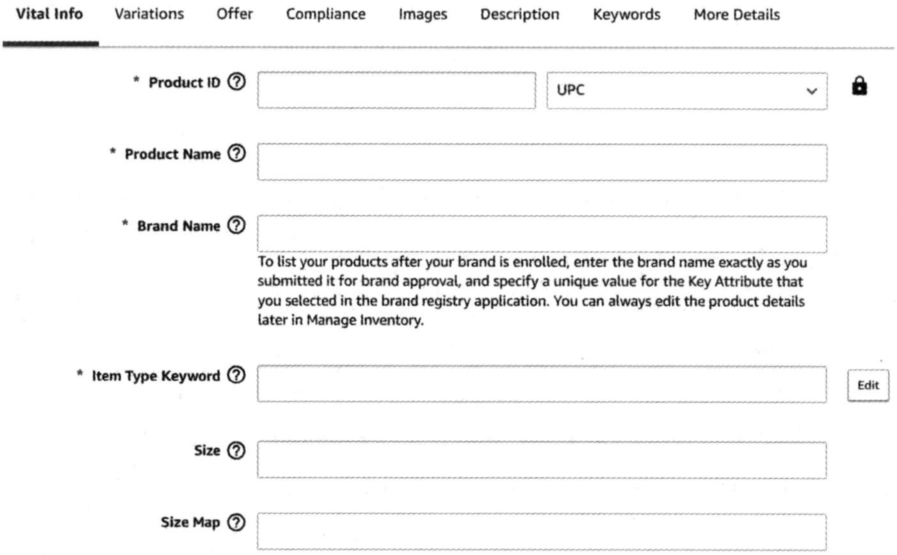

Fig. 4-9　Vital Info

Offer

Next, let's move to the "Offer" tab. This is where you will notate your selling price, create your custom SKU, provide a Condition, and note how this listing's inventory will be fulfilled (Fig. 4-10). If you do not create a SKU yourself, Amazon will create one for you that is a long alpha-numeric string. If your brand does not already have a SKU naming system, we highly recommend you create a system now before you create any listings.

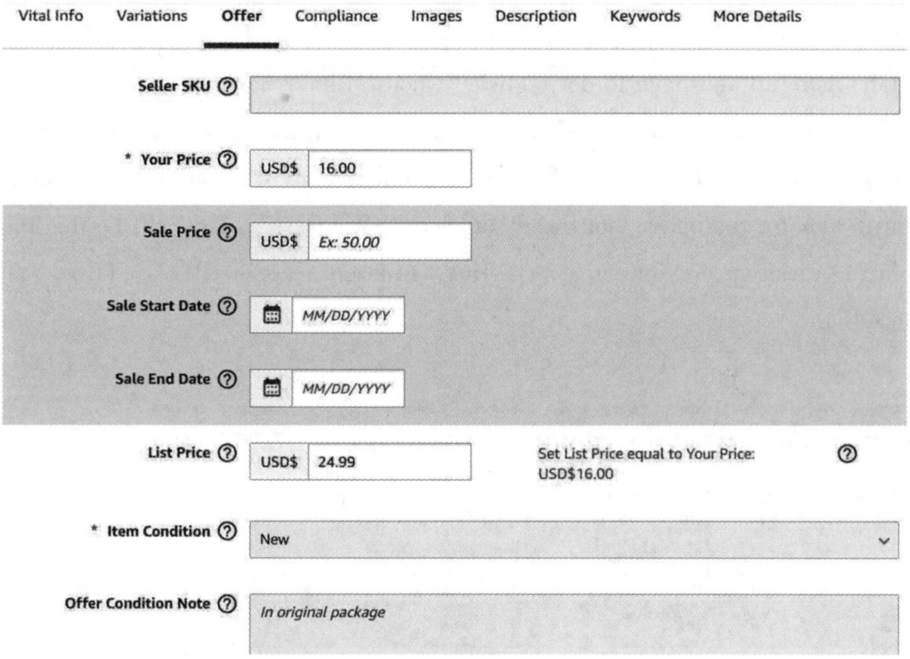

Fig. 4-10 Offer

Compliance

The "Compliance" tab is the area where you can provide any battery information (if relevant) to your product, note warnings like "Prop 65", and a "Safety Data Sheet" if that pertains to your product type (Fig. 4-11).

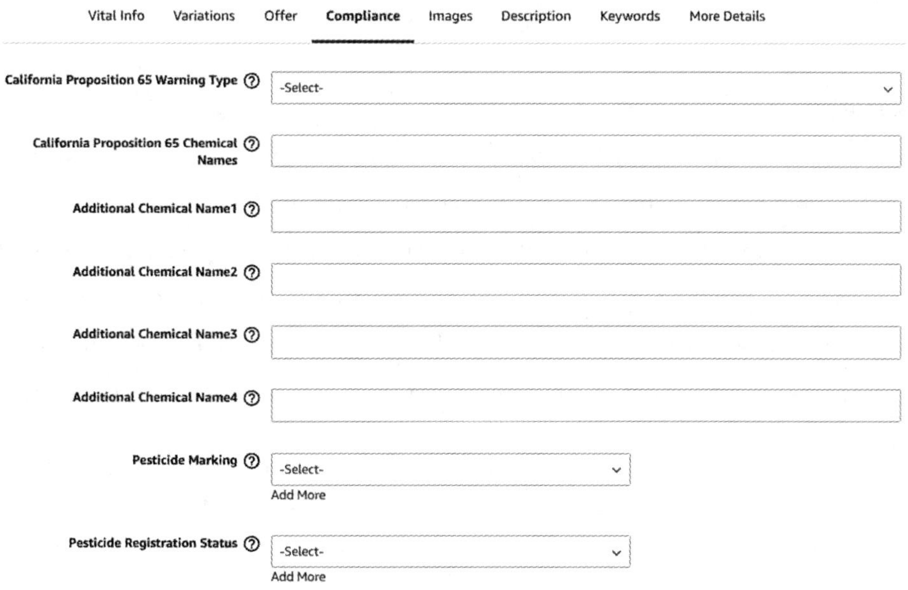

Fig. 4-11 Compliance

Images

In the "Images" tab, you can submit up to nine images (Fig. 4-12). This is a rather intuitive tab where all you have to do is click "Choose file", navigate to where your images are located on your computer and select to upload. Most categories permit you to upload up to nine images. If you are uploading images to a product that is a variant of a Parent-Child relationship, look for the image slot that is labeled "SWATCH". This will be the image that displays in the variation preview on your listing. Amazon accepts JPEGs, TIFFs, and non-animation GIFs.

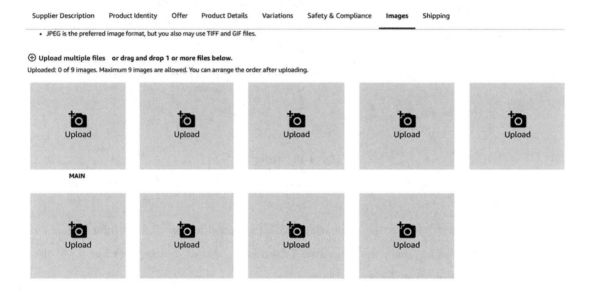

Fig. 4-12　Images

Description

The "Description" tab is what contains the "meat" of your listing; this is where most of your optimized product copy should live (Fig. 4-13). The product description field permits up to 2,000 characters to be submitted. Initially, you will only see one "Key Product Features" field, so you must click the link "Add More" to provide more fields, to a maximum of five. The character permitted in the "Key Product Features" fields fluctuate between categories, so it is best to hover over the information "i" badge to see what your current category permits.

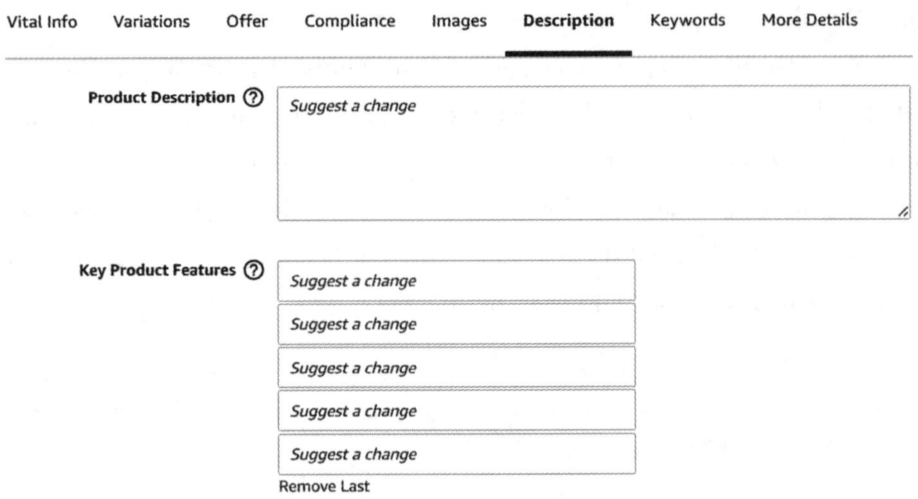

Fig. 4-13　Description

Keywords

The "Keywords" tab is full of fields that help improve the discoverability of your product listings, but do not display on your listing anywhere (Fig. 4-14). Similar to the "Key Product Features", you can have up to five fields on most of these, but you must click the "Add More" link to make them all appear. Focus on the "Search Terms" field, as it allows you to add up to 500 characters of keywords you might not have published on the front-end of the listing.

4-4　关键词的作用

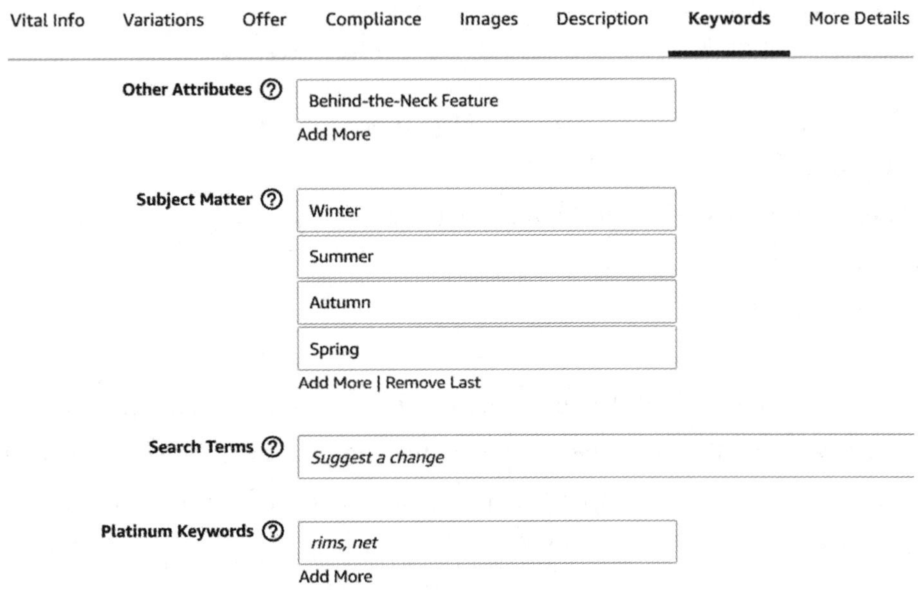

Fig. 4-14　Keywords

More Details

The "More Details" tab is where all of your nitty-gritty product specifications live (Fig. 4-15). This is a relatively self-explanatory tab, but you will see there could be a lot of fields that do not relate to your product. Amazon generalizes what fields might be needed based on your category, so do not feel pressure to fill out all fields. We recommend screening through all fields and filling out the relatable ones, but below are the minimum requirement fields to create your listing for Fulfillment by Amazon:

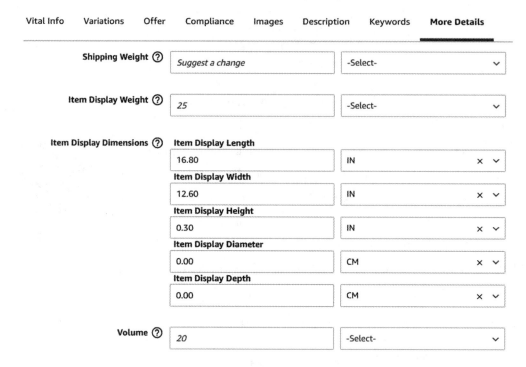

Fig. 4-15　More Details

(1) Weight;

(2) Item Dimensions—Length, Width, Height;

(3) Unit Count;

(4) Unit Count Type.

Once you have input all of the above suggested fields, you are now ready to "Save and finish" your new product listing. Once you click this button, Amazon will assign an Amazon Standard Identification Number (ASIN) and you can almost immediately see what your new listing looks like.

Exercises

I. Put the information in the right category.

1. UPC
2. appliances
3. sale price
4. brand name
5. sale time
6. baby products
7. JPEGs
8. TIFFs
9. key product features
10. product ID
11. product name
12. your price
13. battery average life
14. non-animation GIFs
15. color
16. handling time
17. product description
18. target audience
19. status
20. cell phones & accessories
21. manufacturer
22. SKU
23. length
24. other attributes
25. search terms
26. size
27. weight
28. numbers

A. Category_____

B. Vital Info_____

C. Offer_____

D. Compliance_____

E. Images_____

F. Description_____

G. Keywords_____

H. More Details_____

Ⅱ. **Finish the product listing information chart in English as required according to the information provided below.**

产品名称	运动背包	产品分类	体育及户外>户外休闲装备>背包
UPC	526664585585	品牌及制造商	ETUDE
制造商零件编号	FE	原产国/地区	China
颜色	黑色	价格	39.99 USD
SKU	GYMBAG-BLACK01	处理时间	5
销售数量	30	状况	全新
产品描述	该运动包有一个宽的主口袋和八个独立的口袋,两个前袋和一个内湿袋;侧边网状口袋可放一个水瓶,内袋可放洗发水和洗面奶		
五点描述（其一）	底部采用防水、耐磨的皮革	适用人群	男女通用
尺寸	20*10*10 英寸	重量	500g

Product Listing Information

Category _____	Sports and Outdoors>Sports & Outdoor Recreation Accessories>Gym Bags	
_____	product name	
	brand name	
	product ID	
	manufacturer	
	color	

continued Table

	price	
	SKU	
_____	status	
	numbers	
	handling time	
_____	product description	
	one of key product features	
	target audience	
_____	other attributes	
	search terms	
_____	weight	
	size	

 Notes for 1+X Certificate

Amazon's Image Requirements

If you want to be successful on Amazon, you have to play by Amazon's rules—especially when it comes to product images. The last thing you want is for Amazon to suppress your listing because you have violated the image requirements.

Amazon's full list of image requirements is as follows.

(1) Images must accurately represent the product and show only the product that is for sale.

(2) The product and all its features must be clearly visible.

(3) MAIN images should have a pure white background (pure white blends in with the Amazon search and product detail pages—RGB color values of 255, 255, 255).

(4) MAIN images must be professional photographs of the actual product (graphics, illustrations, mockups, or placeholders are not allowed). They must not show excluded accessories; props that might confuse the customer; text that is not part of the product; or logos, watermarks, or inset images.

(5) Images must match the product title.

(6) Images should be 1,600 pixels or larger on the longest side. This minimum size requirement enables the zoom function on the website. Zoom has been proven to enhance sales.

(7) Images must not exceed 10,000 pixels on the longest side.

(8) Amazon accepts JPEG (.jpeg), TIFF (.tiff) or GIF (.gif) file formats, but JPEG is preferred.

(9) Amazon does not support animated gifs.

(10) Images must not contain nudity or be sexually suggestive.

(11) MAIN images of shoes should be of a single shoe, facing left at a 45-degree angle.

(12) Women's and Men's Clothing MAIN images should be photographed on a model.

(13) All Kids & Baby Clothing images should be photographed flat (off-model).

The MAIN Amazon Product Image

If your MAIN image does not resemble the above, Amazon may suppress your listing, and your product will be inactive. Here are some prohibited features for main images.

(1) Product images should not include any Amazon logos or trademarks, or variations, modifications or anything confusingly similar to Amazon's logos and trademarks. This includes, but is not limited to, any words or logos with the terms AMAZON, PRIME, ALEXA, or the Amazon Smile design.

(2) Product images should not include any badges used on Amazon, or variations, modifications or anything confusingly similar to such badges. This includes, but is not limited to, "Amazon's Choice", "Premium Choice", "Amazon Alexa", "Works with Amazon Alexa", or "Best Seller". Refer to trademark usage guidelines for more details.

(3) No nudity or sexually suggestive images.

(4) Product images should not be blurry, pixelated, or have jagged edges.

(5) Product should not take up less than 85% of the entire image.

Task 5 Title Description

 Project Description

In order to get products searched quickly, a good title is vital. Therefore, as an operations specialist, you will need to write successful product titles.

 Project Requirement

· Write correct product titles.

 Learning Goals

· Understand the criteria for product titles on Amazon.
· Master the title formats in different product categories and write correct Amazon product titles.
· Master words and expressions related to title description.

Module One   Warm-up

Look at the following picture, and please help to choose one appropriate title for this product.

A. Mkeke Magnetic Designed for iPhone 14 Pro Case Clear with MagSafe Shockproof Phone Case for Apple iPhone 14 Pro 2022.

B. FREE SHIPPING & NEW ARRIVAL !!! Mkeke Magnetic Designed for iPhone 14 Pro Case Clear with MagSafe Shockproof Phone Case.

C. MOZOTER magnetic case for iPhone 14 Pro Case, 3 Pcs glass screen protector and camera lens protector, shockproof slim phone case cover 6.1"-Clear.

Module Two   Reading

Product Title Requirements

Title requirements apply to all products on all of Amazon's worldwide marketplaces. The four criteria for product title are as follows.

(1) Titles must follow the recommended length of your product category characters, including spaces.

(2) Titles must not contain promotional phrases, such as "free shipping", "100% quality guaranteed".

(3) Titles must not contain characters for decoration, such as ~ ! * $? _ ~ { } # < >| * ; ^ ¬ | etc.

(4) Titles must contain product-identifying information, such as "hiking boots" or "umbrella".

Failure to comply with these requirements may cause a product to be suppressed from Amazon search results.

Good title quality is a key factor in ensuring a positive customer experience on Amazon (Fig. 5-1). Below are additional tips for improving the quality of your titles, and we strongly encourage adherence to the following title standards.

Fig. 5-1 Title with Product-identifying Information

(1) Titles should be concise. We recommend fewer than 80 characters.

(2) Do not use ALL CAPS.

(3) Capitalize the first letter of each word except for prepositions (in, on, over, with), conjunctions (and, or, for), or articles (the, a, an).

(4) Use numerals: "2" instead of "two".

(5) Don not use non-language ASCII characters such as Æ, ©, or ®.

(6) Titles should contain the minimal information needed to identify the item and nothing more.

(7) Do not use subjective commentary, such as "Hot Item" or "Best Seller".

(8) Titles can include necessary punctuation, like hyphens (-), forward slashes (/), commas (,), ampersands (&), and periods (.).

(9) Titles can abbreviate measurements, such as "cm", "oz", "in", and "kg".

(10) Do not include your merchant name in titles.

(11) Size and color variations should be included in titles for child ASINs, not the main title.

Titles usually use variation relationships (Fig. 5-2). In variation relationships, child ASIN titles may appear on the detail page once the child ASIN is selected, so it is important to include the variation attributes like size and color in the title for the child ASIN.

5-1 介绍父、子 ASIN

Fig. 5-2 Product Title Using Variation Relationships

Example parent: Crocs Beach Clog.

Example child: Crocs Beach Clog, Lime Green, Men's Size 8-9.

Research shows that customers scan-read results, meaning that titles do not need to contain the exact phrase that customers are searching for in order to catch their eye. Longer titles are also harder to read than shorter titles, so the longer your title is, the more you risk losing your customer's attention.

Think about a physical product on a supermarket shelf. Its title is simple and to the point. You only have a moment to catch the eye of a passing shopper. With online titles on Amazon, there's no need to go on and on. Simply put, the title should reflect what is on the physical packaging of a product.

New Words and Expressions

requirement /rɪˈkwaɪəmənt/ n. 必要条件；必备的条件

criterion /kraɪˈtɪərɪən/ n. 标准

length /leŋθ/ n. 长度

promotional /prəˈməʊʃənl/ adj. 广告宣传的；推销的

decoration /ˌdekəˈreɪʃn/ n. 装饰品

suppress /səˈpres/ v. 阻止；抑制

ensure /ɪnˈʃʊə(r)/ v. 确保
additional /əˈdɪʃənl/ adj. 额外的
violate /ˈvaɪəleɪt/ v. 违反
adherence /ədˈhɪərəns/ n. 遵守；遵循
concise /kənˈsaɪs/ adj. 简明的
capitalize /ˈkæpɪtəlaɪz/ v. 把……首字母大写
preposition /ˌprepəˈzɪʃn/ n. 介词
conjunction /kənˈdʒʌŋkʃn/ n. 连词
article /ˈɑːtɪkl/ n. 冠词
numeral /ˈnjuːmərəl/ n. 数字
identify /aɪˈdentɪfaɪ/ v. 确认；认出
subjective /səbˈdʒektɪv/ adj. 主观的
commentary /ˈkɒməntri/ n. 评论
punctuation /ˌpʌŋktʃuˈeɪʃn/ n. 标点符号
comma /ˈkɒmə/ n. 逗号
ampersand /ˈæmpəsænd/ n. 表示 and 的符号
abbreviate /əˈbriːvieɪt/ v. 缩写
measurement /ˈmeʒəmənt/ n. 度量
variation /ˌveəriˈeɪʃn/ n. 变体
attribute /əˈtrɪbjuːt/ n. 属性
comply with 遵守
forward slash 正斜杠
catch one's eye 引起……的注意

Terms

ASCII (American Standard Code for Information Interchange)　美国信息交换标准代码
ASIN (Amazon Standard Identification Number)　亚马逊标准商品编码
merchant name　店铺名称
child ASIN　子 ASIN
detail page　详情页

Exercises

I. Write T for true or F for false in the brackets beside the following statements about the text.

1. All products on Amazon platform must comply with the four criteria for product titles. ( )
2. For attracting more buyers, you'd better add words like "buy one and get one free" in the title. ( )
3. Information which could help customers to identify the product should be contained in the title. ( )
4. The search of one product will be suppressed if its title does not follow the requirements. ( )
5. A long title with more key words is better. ( )
6. Capital letters should not be used in the title. ( )
7. Any symbol or punctuation was not allowed for a good title. ( )
8. "Adidas Men's Kaptir 2.0 Running Shoe" does not comply with Amazon's title requirements because merchant name "Adidas" should not be included. ( )
9. "Best seller" should not be contained in the title. ( )
10. Size and color variations usually appear on the detail page. ( )

II. Read the text again and fill in the blanks in the following sentences.

1. All products on all of Amazon's worldwide marketplaces must follow _____.
2. As mentioned in the four criteria, titles of amazon products must not contain _____ and _____.
3. Failure to follow the title requirements may have a negative impact on the _____ of a product.
4. Apart from the four criteria, this passage also strongly encourages adherence to some _____.
5. Don't use all caps, _____ or _____ in titles.
6. Titles can include necessary punctuation, like _____ (-), _____ (/), _____ (,), ampersands (&), and periods (.).
7. It is important to include the _____ like size and color in the title for the child ASIN.

8. Longer titles are also harder to read than shorter titles, so the _____ your title is, the _____ you risk losing your customer's attention.

III. Translate the following passage into Chinese.

Research shows that customers scan-read results, meaning that titles do not need to contain the exact phrase that customers are searching for in order to catch their eye. Longer titles are also harder to read than shorter titles, so the longer your title is, the more you risk losing your customer's attention.

Module Three　Project Implementation

How to Write Amazon Product Titles That Drive Clicks

Copywriting is the art of creating advertising and marketing messages that persuade someone to take action. For Amazon product titles, that action is likely to be a click.

When someone searches for "AA Batteries" in the marketplace, it will be the photo, the price, and a product title that differentiates between more than 40 products on just the first page of results.

An Amazon search results page, like many e-commerce product search results pages, shows relatively little information. There is a product photograph, a price, a Prime badge, and the product's title (Fig. 5-3). The photograph gives the shopper an idea of the product. The price is a point of comparison, and the title often confirms the product's type, specifications, and brand. The title's role in the persuasion process is to provide information.

5-2　亚马逊 Prime 会员

Consider some of the product titles for AA batteries.

"Energizer AA Batteries (48 Count) Double A Max Alkaline Battery"

"ACDelco AA Super Alkaline Batteries in Reclosable Package, 100 Count"

"Amazon Basics AA 1.5 Volt Performance Alkaline Batteries-Pack of 48"

"Rayovac AA Batteries, Alkaline Double-A Batteries (72 Battery Count)"

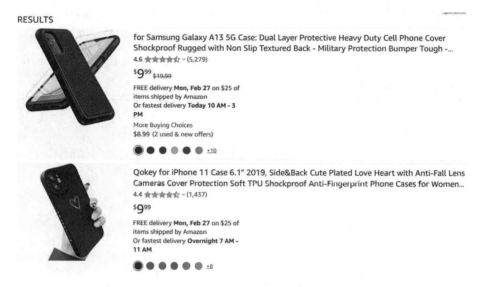

Fig. 5-3　Amazon Search Results Page

These product titles tell the shopper the brand name, the product type, an optional detail, and how many batteries are included for the price (Fig. 5-4). Although the exact order of these elements differs slightly, the pattern is as below.

Fig. 5-4　More Examples about Product Titles for AA Batteries

Brand | Type | Detail | Count

Take, for example, "ACDelco AA Super Alkaline Batteries in Reclosable Package, 100 Count."

Brand: ACDelco

Type: AA Super Alkaline Batteries

Detail: in Reclosable Package

Count: 100 Count

In combination with the price and photograph, these titles confirm to the shopper what she is getting, and, thereby, enable the click to the product page to consummate the purchase.

When you write Amazon product titles, look for patterns similar to the one described for AA batteries within your product's Amazon category. It is important to note that not all products require the same content in their titles. For example, the title for a computer (Fig. 5-5) would be significantly more detailed than the information for a T-shirt (Fig. 5-6). Table 5-1 includes a few of the recommended formats in different product categories.

Lenovo 2022 Newest Ideapad 3 Laptop, 15.6" HD Touchscreen, 11th Gen Intel Core i3-1115G4 Processor, 8GB DDR4 RAM, 256GB PCIe NVMe SSD, HDMI, Webcam, Wi-Fi 5, Bluetooth, Windows 11 Home, Almond

Visit the Lenovo Store

☆☆☆☆☆ ∨   1,786 ratings | 167 answered questions

#1 Best Seller in Traditional Laptop Computers

-60% $384⁰⁰

List Price: $959.00

$76.86 Shipping & Import Fees Deposit to China Details ∨
Available at a lower price from other sellers that may not offer free Prime shipping.

Capacity: **8GB RAM | 256GB SSD**

| 4GB RAM | 128GB SSD | 8GB RAM | 256GB SSD |
| 6 options from $330.00 | $384.00 |

Fig. 5-5   A Product Title for Computers

Showing results for *plain t shirt*
Search instead for PLAIN T SHIRT

RESULTS
Price and other details may vary based on product size and color.

Featured from our brands
Goodthreads Men's Slim-Fit Short-Sleeve Cotton Crewneck T-Shirt
4.3 ★★★★☆ (10,491)
Amazon brand

Sponsored
Saloogoe Womens Loose Fit Tshirts Short Sleeve Summer Tops Casual Workout Yoga Tunic T Shirts Tops
4.4 ★★★★☆ (1,718)
$19⁹⁹
Ships to China

Fig. 5-6　Product Titles for T-shirts

Table 5-1　Recommended Formats of Products Title

Product Type	Title Style
Cookware & Cutlery	Brand + Line + Size + Product Type
Small Appliances	Brand + Model Number + Model Name + Product Type, Color
Video Games	Brand + Model Number + Product Type + Platform
Bedding	Brand + Line/Pattern + Thread Count + Material + Size + Product Type, Color
Bath Towels	Brand + Line/Pattern + Material + Product Type + Quantity, Color
Laptop/Desktop Computers	Brand + Model Number + PC Type + (Processor Speed + MB RAM + Hard Drive Size + Optical Drive)

Exercises

Ⅰ. Please answer the following questions based on the passage.

1. What is the function of copywriting of a product?

2. What information can an Amazon search results page offer to buyers?
_____

3. What is the role of a title on the Amazon search results page?
_____

4. From the passage, we can note that not all products require the same content in their titles. Can you add the title style of TVs to the table above?
_____

II. Please analyze the given title as the following example.

Example:

<u>ACDelco</u> <u>AA Super Alkaline Batteries</u> in <u>Reclosable Package</u>, <u>100 Count</u>.
 |Brand| |Type| |Detail| |Count|

Please analyze the following title.

<u>LEVOIT</u> <u>Classic300S</u> <u>Ultrasonic Smart Top Fill Humidifier</u>, <u>Extra Large 4L Tank</u> for
 □   □   □   □

Whole Family, <u>APP & Voice Control</u>, <u>Humidity Setting with Sensor</u>, <u>Quiet Sleep Mode</u>,
                                                                    □

<u>Blue</u>.
□

III. **Please combine the information given below into a suitable title for the following product.**

Information for this product:

Greeno	wall mount	espresso
6 tier	radial	corner shelf
7.8"D x 7.8"W x 48.8"H		

Title of this product:
_____

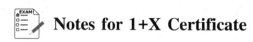

Notes for 1+X Certificate

Optimizing the Amazon Product Title

For a successful marketing of your product, you should optimize the product listing especially with regard to Amazon SEO (Search Engine Optimization). There are a few things to consider. The optimization already starts with the Amazon product title. This is not only part of what a potential customer sees first in the search queries, but the keywords contained in it play an important role in the findability of the product on Amazon.

The product title is especially important for the Amazon search algorithm A9. The search words or keywords placed in the product title have an influence on the relevance of your product. The title is therefore one of the most important sources of keywords for the search algorithm. If possible, write 2-3 main keywords in a meaningful phrase in your title.

In addition, the product title should attract the attention of the customer on the one hand, and on the other hand, it should prove to be sales-promoting. So think about what makes your product stand out and how it differs from your competitors. This could be a certain material, a special color or a special function. Put yourself in the shoes of your potential customers when you are searching for a title. A title that consists only of a series of search terms does not look appealing.

We recommend that you use the Amazon Style Guide as a guide so that you do not run the risk of your product being hidden. Also, when creating your product title, do not forget to use the mobile view so that your product title can be displayed there in full length.

Task 6　Product Description

 Project Description

Product description is an important part of Amazon product listing which is a good way for sellers to advertise their products and boost sales on Amazon. As an operations specialist, you will need to write compelling Amazon product description.

 Project Requirement

· Write Amazon product description.

 Learning Goals

· Understand the key points of product description on Amazon.
· Understand the components of product description template.
· Master how to write bullet points.
· Master words and expressions related to product description.

Module One Warm-up

Suppose you need to buy a new school bag on Amazon for your daily classes, what information do you expect from the product description?

```
Product Information




```

 ## Module Two Reading

Amazon Product Description

If your product is directly competing with a product listed on Amazon, it is time to create your product listing in Seller Central. A report by Wunderman Thompson Commerce highlights that sixty-three percent of consumers start their online shopping searches on Amazon in key e-commerce markets.

Amazon's platform removes the pain points of customer acquisition. Your brand becomes a part of a buyer's journey from the beginning with Amazon's vast and loyal customer base. According to research by JP Morgan, Amazon is on track to be the largest U.S. retailer in 2022 and will overtake Walmart. Your brand's success on Amazon, however, relies on your understanding and ability to write Amazon product descriptions that do three things: catch buyers' attention, convince them that your product is the best choice, and convert them into customers through purchases and subscriptions (Fig. 6-1).

Amazon's Seller Central offers a wealth of knowledge to set sellers up for success. Maybe even more importantly, it shares exactly what Amazon wants and requires for product descriptions and listings (Fig. 6-2). Your product description should assist the customer in understanding your product, and more importantly, its unique features and benefits.

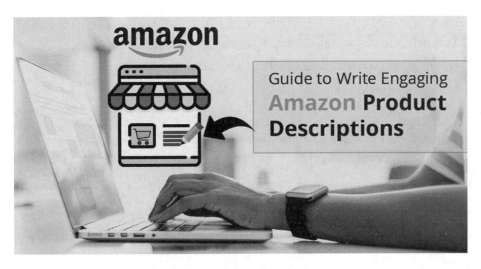

Fig. 6-1　Product Description

Price	$10.75	$13.97	$29.97	$7.99
Shipping	√Prime	√Prime	√Prime	√Prime
Sold By	Integrity Sales LLC	di Oro Living	di Oro Living	Amazon.com
Color	Stainless Steel	Dark Bronze	Dark Bronze	Gray
Material Type	Silicone	Silicone	Silicone	Silicone
	Add to Cart	Add to Cart	Add to Cart	Add to Cart

Please help us improve this feature. Tell us what you think of this feature.

Product Description

Size: Large

The OXO Good Grips Silicone Flexible Turners combine the strength of stainless steel with the advantages of silicone. The silicone outer layer, which is heat resistant to 600 degrees Fahrenheit and safe for non-stick cookware, is bonded to a flexible stainless steel core for added stability. The Turners have thin, flexible edges that glide easily beneath all foods and are perfect for flipping fragile foods while keeping them intact. Use the Large Silicone Flexible Turner can be used to flip eggs, burgers, crepes and more. All Silicone Flexible Turners have soft, comfortable, non-slip grips and are the perfect companions to non-stick cookware and bakeware.

Product Information

Size:Large

Product Dimensions	3.8 x 3.5 x 12.8 inches
Item Weight	4.8 ounces
Shipping Weight	4.8 ounces (View shipping rates and policies)
Department	unisex
Manufacturer	OXO Cook's Tools
ASIN	B000JPVCYE
Item model number	1071534
Customer Reviews	1,320 customer reviews 4.5 out of 5 stars
Best Sellers Rank	#352 in Home & Kitchen (See Top 100 in Home & Kitchen) #4 in Kitchen & Dining > Kitchen Utensils & Gadgets > Cooking Utensils > Spatulas
Date first available at Amazon.com	October 17, 2006

Feedback

Would you like to give feedback on images?
Would you like to tell us about a lower price?

Related Video Shorts

Page 1 of 2

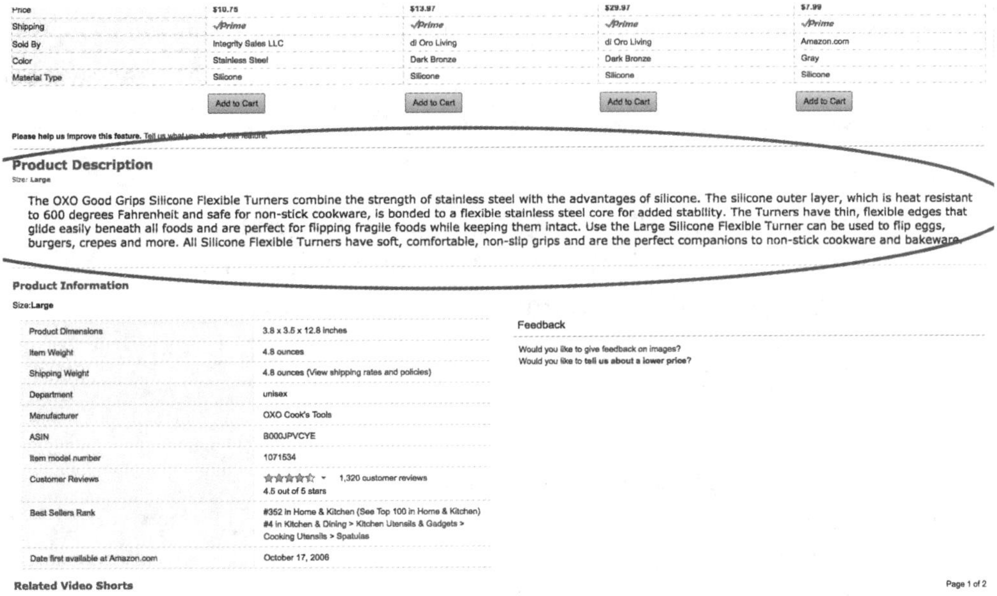

Fig. 6-2　Example of Product Description

Here are some key points Amazon highlights that a product description should be like as follows.

(1) A concise, honest, and friendly overview of your product's uses and where it fits in its category.

(2) Features and benefits of the product and a focus on its unique properties.

(3) Written clearly and concisely to help customers understand the product.

(4) Reviews the best applications for the product.

(5) Grammatically sound before submission.

(6) Competitors should not be mentioned or included.

(7) Text only with a limited number of characters.

(8) Follow all of Amazon's standards.

An Amazon product description cannot be like this.

(1) Stuff keywords.

(2) Compare your product to competitors or plagiarize their listings.

(3) Promote your external website.

(4) Write long descriptions of the details of your product.

(5) Include details about your company or other products you sell.

Amazon is also very clear about how they want their sellers to format their product descriptions.

Amazon's product description template includes three sections.

(1) A product title: This should be kept to 200 characters (preferably less).

(2) A bullet points section: It is one of the important sections where you can describe the selling features of the product in detail (Fig. 6-3).

RUIDESUN 2 Pack Magnetic Picture Collage Frame for Refrigerator, Each Frame Holds 1 6x8 Inch and 6 4x6 Inch Photos, Total 14 Photos, Black
Brand: RUIDESUN

Currently unavailable.
We don't know when or if this item will be back in stock.

Brand	RUIDESUN
Number of Items	2
Unit Count	2.0 Count

About this item
- Bigger capacity: 7 pictures for each magnetic photo collage frame, one 6x8 inch and six 4x6 inch photos.
- Protective: a good protector to your photos. They will be bright and clean for years inside the frame.
- Show your quality time: a wonderful decoration to your fridge, turn it into a wonderful display of your quality times
- Easy to use: easy to put in and take out your pictures any time you want. You can stick them to your fridge and move them freely to any part you like, vertically and horizontally.
- Popular: a wonderful gift for spacial days like, Mother's day, Christmas, Wedding, Birthdays, Anniversaries etc.

Fig. 6-3 Bullet Points

(3) The main product description section: Your product description is where you tell a story about how your product will benefit the buyer. This is where you can expand on your key product features, and include additional features and benefits about your product that the buyer will care about. This section allows up to 2,000 characters that follow the above guidelines.

New Words and Expressions

highlight /ˈhaɪlaɪt/ v. 突出；强调
remove /rɪˈmuːv/ v. 去除
acquisition /ˌækwɪˈzɪʃn/ n. 获得；得到
vast /vɑːst/ adj. 大量的
loyal /ˈlɔɪəl/ adj. 忠诚的
overtake /ˌəʊvəˈteɪk/ v. 超过；赶上
convince /kənˈvɪns/ v. 使相信
convert /kənˈvɜːt/ v. 转变；转化
assist /əˈsɪst/ v. 帮助；协助
overview /ˈəʊvəvjuː/ n. 概述；概况
property /ˈprɒpəti/ n. 性质；特性
application /ˌæplɪˈkeɪʃn/ n. 应用，运用
sound /saʊnd/ adj. 正确的
submission /səbˈmɪʃn/ n. 提交
stuff /stʌf/ v. 填满；装满
plagiarize /ˈpleɪdʒəraɪz/ v. 剽窃
template /ˈtempleɪt/ n. 样板；模板
be on track 稳步前进
rely on 依靠
convert into 转化为
pain point 痛点

Terms

product listing   产品页面

Seller Central   卖家平台

customer acquisition   客户体验

bullet points   五点描述

Exercises

I. Write T for true or F for false in the brackets beside the following statements about the text.

1. Sellers have to create a product listing if they want to compete with other similar products on Amazon. ( )
2. Amazon had become the largest retailer in the world. ( )
3. Converting website visitors into consumers is an important factor for a brand's success. ( )
4. It is difficult for sellers to get any help from Amazon platform. ( )
5. The most important factor for a product description is pictures in high quality. ( )
6. The product description should be as long as possible. ( )
7. You'd better not mention competitors in your product description. ( )
8. The more keywords there are, the better the product description is. ( )
9. 200 characters were allowed for the main section of product description. ( )
10. There are three parts in a complete product description. ( )

II. Read the text again and fill in the blanks in the following sentences.

1. Three things have to be done when you write Amazon product descriptions, including _____, _____, _____ through purchases and subscriptions.
2. Your product description should help buyers to understand your product better, especially focusing on its unique _____ and _____.
3. A product description should be a _____, honest, and friendly _____ of your product's uses and where it fits in its category.
4. Before you submit your product description please check whether there is any _____ mistake.
5. It is not a good idea to _____ your competitors' listings.
6. An Amazon product description is not a place to include details about your _____ or _____ you sell.

7. Amazon's product description template includes three sections: _____ , _____ , and _____ .

III. Translate the following passage into Chinese.

Amazon is on track to be the largest U. S. retailer in 2022 and will overtake Walmart. Your brand's success on Amazon, however, relies on your understanding and ability to write Amazon product descriptions that do three things: catch buyers' attention, convince them that your product is the best choice, and convert them into customers through purchases and subscriptions.

Module Three Project Implementation

How to Add and Write Amazon Bullet Points

Sellers can include bullet points while creating or editing Amazon product listings. Please follow these steps.

(1) Sign in to Seller Central, and go to your product listing.

(2) Once in the Manage Inventory page, click on "Edit".

(3) Open the "Description" tab, and go to "Key Product Features".

(4) Select "Add more" to submit your bullet points in the 5 key features fields available (Fig. 6-4).

This is only the final step in the process. Now, let's review what it takes to create effective Amazon points. Great bullet points follow Amazon's guidelines, but they also go the extra mile. Remember, you have a very limited space to delight users. So, every word has got to count. Here are 4 tips to help you create great Amazon bullet points.

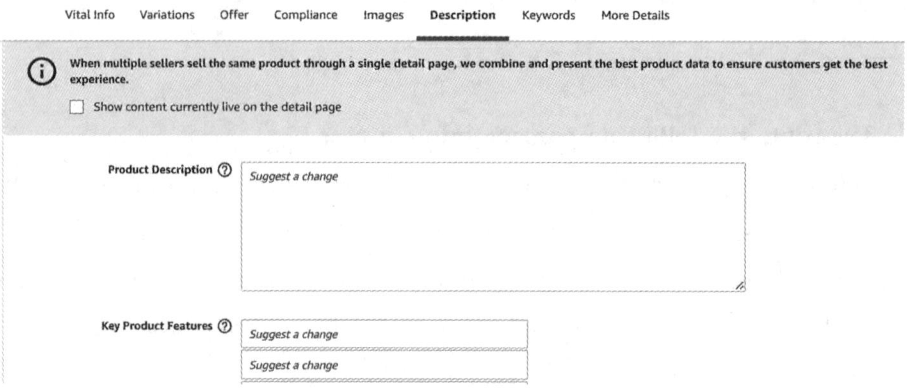

Fig. 6-4　Add Bullet Points

1. Search Engine Optimization

You have heard about the Amazon A9 algorithm. This AI tool reviews several areas of your product listings to rank them on Amazon search. One of the most important tenets is keywords.

6-1　介绍 SEO

Amazon customers use keywords to find specific items in the marketplace. The better the keyword match, the better chance they have of finding your products.

But do not try to stuff your bullets with as many terms as possible. Go about it the creative way.

(1) Select 10 to 20 highly relevant keywords to use on Amazon bullet points;

(2) Try to use one to two keywords per sentence, and make them fit in an organic way, so customers can have an easy read;

(3) Avoid repetition, it is not necessary to repeat keywords in a single space, in fact, Amazon may flag our listings when you do this;

(4) Try to put keywords in high-ranking areas, for example, a listing that has a keyword in its title will perform better than if the keyword was in the description.

(5) It is crucial to make the most of your keywords in Amazon bullet points. That will improve your search placement in the marketplace (Fig. 6-5).

2. Deliver Great Content

The Amazon A9 algorithm favors product listings with high-conversion rates (Fig. 6-6), but it takes more than SEO to make a sale. This is where great content makes a difference.

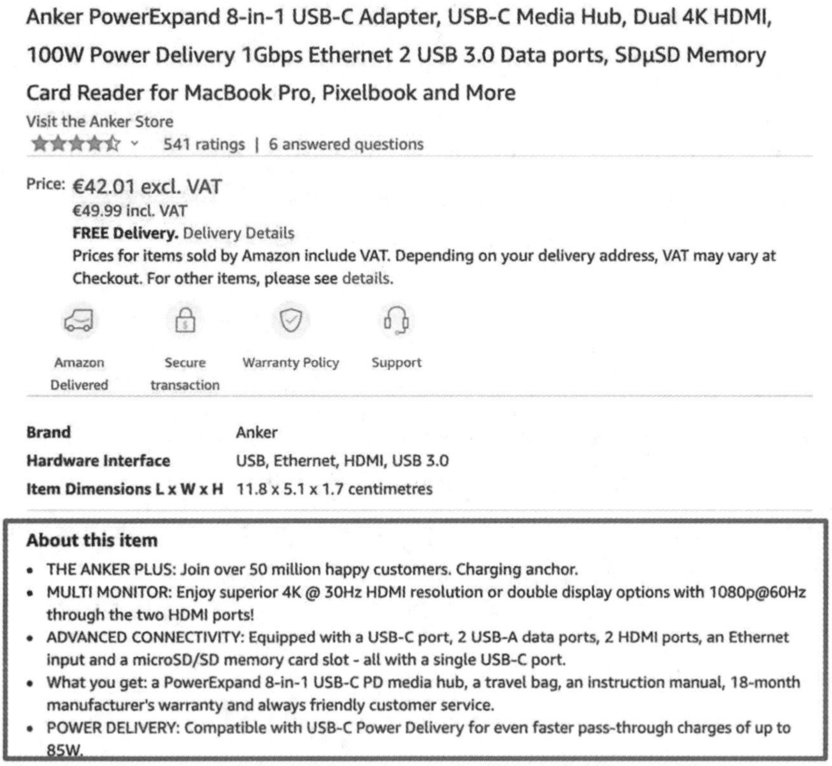

Anker PowerExpand 8-in-1 USB-C Adapter, USB-C Media Hub, Dual 4K HDMI, 100W Power Delivery 1Gbps Ethernet 2 USB 3.0 Data ports, SDμSD Memory Card Reader for MacBook Pro, Pixelbook and More
Visit the Anker Store
541 ratings | 6 answered questions
Price: €42.01 excl. VAT
€49.99 incl. VAT
FREE Delivery. Delivery Details
Prices for items sold by Amazon include VAT. Depending on your delivery address, VAT may vary at Checkout. For other items, please see details.
Amazon Delivered
Secure transaction
Warranty Policy
Support
Brand Anker
Hardware Interface USB, Ethernet, HDMI, USB 3.0
Item Dimensions L x W x H 11.8 x 5.1 x 1.7 centimetres
About this item
• THE ANKER PLUS: Join over 50 million happy customers. Charging anchor.
• MULTI MONITOR: Enjoy superior 4K @ 30Hz HDMI resolution or double display options with 1080p@60Hz through the two HDMI ports!
• ADVANCED CONNECTIVITY: Equipped with a USB-C port, 2 USB-A data ports, 2 HDMI ports, an Ethernet input and a microSD/SD memory card slot - all with a single USB-C port.
• What you get: a PowerExpand 8-in-1 USB-C PD media hub, a travel bag, an instruction manual, 18-month manufacturer's warranty and always friendly customer service.
• POWER DELIVERY: Compatible with USB-C Power Delivery for even faster pass-through charges of up to 85W.

Fig. 6-5 Bullet Points

REVIEWS
PRICE
A9
PRODUCT TITLE AND DESCRIPTION
SALES HISTORY
PRODUCT IMAGES

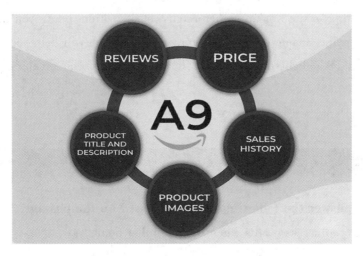

Fig. 6-6 The Amazon A9 Algorithm

Customer delight is your first priority. So, take note of the following tenets when you write your bullet points.

(1) Tell users about the advantages of your offer; deliver some technical details, but also get creative; let customers know how you can help them improve their lives.

(2) Stick to the facts and avoid inflated claims; bullet points should not seem like marketing slogans; do not declare that your product is the best—users will make that decision.

(3) In the same vein, any certification claims must be backed up with visible proof.

Many Amazon users do not read beyond the title and bullet points. That is why it is crucial to deliver as much information as possible from the get-go.

3. Stay within the Character Limit

For the length of all bullet points, Amazon recommends a maximum of 500 characters including spaces. It is also important to keep a similar length between bullet points. Keep it nice, clean and easy to read. And do not leave blank bullet points.

Sticking to short, on-point messages improves readability. Not only that, but customers will learn about your product's best highlights in only a few seconds.

4. Market Research

Search for your competitors' listings on Amazon and read their bullet points. Take note of the product features they highlight.

To take things further, compare the bullet points with off-Amazon content. Go into the product manufacturer's site, or any other retail website. From here, you can filter out the most used bullet points among the competition. This approach will help you narrow down the features you should highlight to customers. It will also help you organize your own bullet points.

Exercises

I. Please answer the following questions based on the passage.

1. How will you use keywords when writing bullet points?

2. What information should you focus on to make the content of bullet points great?

3. How to balance the length of bullet points?

II. Please complete the bullet points writing steps based on your own understanding of the text.

Step 1	Search for your competitors' listings on Amazon and read their _____. Take note of the _____ they highlight.
Step 2	Compare the bullet points with off-Amazon content. Go into the _____'s site, or any other _____.
Step 3	Filter out _____ bullet points among the competition.
Step 4	Select the_____ you should highlight to customers.
Step 5	Select 10 to 20 highly relevant _____ to use on Amazon bullet points.
Step 6	Try to use _____ keywords per sentence.
Step 7	Add the bullet points into product listing page.

III. Please complete the bullet points description of the following product based on the keyword information provided.

Keywords:

pop-up tent	set up in seconds
protection from the sun	three mesh windows
lightweight and portable	fit 3-4 people
side sandbag anchor	ground anchor
improved ventilation	

carry bag 78.8" L × 55.1" W × 51.5" H increase comfort outdoor	simple pop-up design open at the front spacious space

About this item:

· The pop-up beach tent provides protections from the sun and increases comfort outdoor.

· _____
· _____
· _____
· _____

 ## Notes for 1+X Certificate

Amazon Bullet Points: Formatting

The following are some of the general formatting principles you need to follow when you begin to formulate your bullet points.

(1) The word limit for each point is up to 15 words or a maximum of 500 characters. The text cannot exceed this, which is why we emphasize keeping your points brief and without filler. At best, you can make a five-line summary of the key features and benefits your product offers.

(2) Sellers are not allowed to indicate the product's price, company details or shipping information in the bullet points space. This forces you to be creative in how you craft each line.

(3) Make sure the tone does not come across as overly promotional. You should try to stay grounded and state facts, instead of making claims that can not be tested. For instance, saying your brand is the best in the market is a very subjective statement, that rings hollow when you consider how many other brands are saying the same thing.

(4) Try to arrange your list of bullet points in the order of their relevance. Prioritize the most important one to appear on top.

(5) Start every bullet point with a capital letter. Follow a consistent format in general. Random capitalization and inconsistent formatting can be off-putting for shoppers.

(6) You do not have to adhere strictly to punctuation rules if the sentences are hard to follow. The goal is to make things easy for your audience to grasp.

(7) If you do need to separate a phrase within a sentence, use a comma instead of a semicolon. Most importantly, do not end your bullet points with punctuation. They count as characters and are also unnecessary in this context.

(8) Different from Amazon titles, there is no need to capitalize every first word in bullet points, because it can be too distracting. Likewise, you should refrain from using special characters for abbreviations. It comes across as unprofessional.

Supplementary Reading

6-2　为什么跨境电商对中国品牌来说是个好消息

Unit Three

Marketing

Task 7 Marketing Strategy

 Project Description

As a professional advertising campaign planner for Amazon business, you are going to coach your partners to design an appropriate marketing strategy so that they can achieve their business goals.

 Project Requirement

· Create a promotion on Amazon.

 Learning Goals

· Understand the importance of a successful marketing strategy in Amazon business.

· Master the procedure of creating Amazon Promotion, and know how to avoid mistakes many sellers have made before.

· Master words and expressions related to marketing strategy.

Unit Three Marketing

 Module One   Warm-up

Look at the following pictures and think about which marketing platform would be more powerful to increase sales on Amazon.

 Module Two   Reading

Creating the Ultimate Amazon Marketing Strategy

Marketing is always changing and Amazon understands this pretty well (Fig. 7-1). The e-commerce giant features several marketing resources which help sellers rise above the competition. Today, we will help you set up the ultimate Amazon digital marketing strategy to stand out from the crowd.

7-1 介绍数字营销

· **What is Amazon Marketing**

Amazon Marketing comprises a myriad of features, aimed at boosting sellers' success in driving brand awareness and customer loyalty. But how can you create a digital marketing strategy that strengthens these concepts?

91

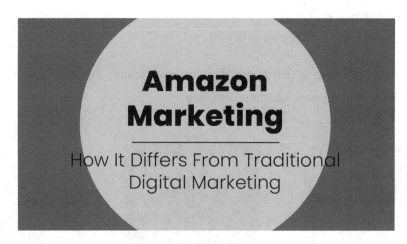

Fig. 7-1　Amazon Marketing

· **There are three main channels to do so**

Amazon SEO: Focused on product listing optimization. SEO (Search Engine Optimization) is used to improve product visibility on Amazon's search results (Fig. 7-2). It is all about keywords. The goal is to use the best search terms to rank higher on search results.

Fig. 7-2　Marketing SEO

There are two types of keywords you can use on Amazon.

Front-end:

They appear on the product title, bullets and description. These are the keywords customers can see. Use them to style up your content and drive sales.

Back-end:

Search terms are hidden within a listing. Customers will not see back-end keywords, but the product will still get a visibility boost.

Amazon Advertising: Relies on Amazon-based tools to create Pay-Per-Click (PPC) ads (Fig. 7-3). It is great for business promotion. Some of the most effective ads are Stores and PPC campaigns. Amazon Advertising provides a visibility boost to your brand and products. It might be expensive, but it can help you boost your visibility, reach more shoppers and increase your sales.

Fig. 7-3 Amazon Ads

Off-Store Marketing: Tools and channels to promote items outside of Amazon. External advertising drives more traffic to Amazon result pages and increases organic ranking. For instance, social media marketing is one of the off-store advertising strategies, which can create a brand community, spread the word about the brand, and then provide feedback that influences future purchase decisions. Besides, there are also many other external marketing plans adopted by sellers like influencer marketing, e-mail marketing (Fig. 7-4), blog marketing and so on.

7-2 介绍网红营销

· **Final Thoughts**

You can select the best tools to design your very own Amazon marketing strategy. Some experts suggest to loop all the marketing activities into the system, believing the cross-channel marketing campaign is more powerful to achieve business goals. And more importantly, you need to create a road map for brand growth and know what campaigns are worth your investment at every stage.

Fig. 7-4 Influencer Marketing

New Words and Expressions

ultimate /ˈʌltɪmət/ adj. 最终的；终极的；最好(或坏、伟大、重要等)的
strategy /ˈstrætədʒi/ n. 策略；计策；行动计划；策划；规划
myriad /ˈmɪriəd/ n. 大量；无数
loyalty /ˈlɔɪəlti/ n. 忠诚；忠实
digital /ˈdɪdʒɪtl/ adj. 数字的；数码的
optimization /ˌɒptɪmaɪˈzeɪʃn/ n. 优化
bullet /ˈbʊlɪt/ n. 子弹；弹丸
external /ɪkˈstɜːnl/ adj. 外部的；外面的
loop /luːp/ v. 使成环；使绕成圈
campaign /kæmˈpeɪn/ n. 运动(为社会、商业或政治目的而进行的一系列有计划的活动)
investment /ɪnˈvestmənt/ n. 投资；投资额；投资物
social media 多媒体
stand out 脱颖而出
style up 装饰，使……个性化
brand awareness 品牌意识
marketing strategy 营销策略

Terms

off-store marketing　站外营销
listing optimization　产品页面优化
Amazon SEO　亚马逊搜索引擎优化
front-end　前端
back-end　后端
Amazon advertising　亚马逊广告
PPC campaign　点击付费广告营销活动
influencer marketing　网红营销
e-mail marketing　电子邮件营销
organic ranking　自然排名；生态排名

Exercises

Ⅰ. **Write T for true or F for false in the brackets beside the following statements about the text.**

1. Marketing is very stable, and it is not a challenge for sellers keep up with trends. 　(　)
2. Amazon Marketing contains many features, aimed at boosting sellers' success in driving brand awareness and customer loyalty. 　(　)
3. The goal of Amazon SEO is to use the best search terms to rank higher on search results. 　(　)
4. There are three types of keywords you can use on Amazon listing optimization including front-end, middle-end and back-end. 　(　)
5. Amazon advertising will cost Amazon sellers nothing at all. 　(　)
6. Amazon PPC ads are very effective. 　(　)
7. Off-store marketing drives more traffic to Amazon result pages and increases organic ranking. 　(　)
8. E-mail advertising is one of external marketing campaigns. 　(　)
9. Some experts believe it is more powerful to use only one marketing campaign to achieve bushiness goal. 　(　)
10. It is important to know what campaigns are worth your investment at every stage. 　(　)

Ⅱ. **Read the text again and fill in the blanks in the following sentences.**

1. Amazon marketing is aimed at boosting sellers' success in driving _____ and _____.

2. There are three main channels to create your Amazon marketing strategy including _____, _____ and _____.

3. Amazon SEO is used to improve product visibility on Amazon's _____. It is all about _____.

4. Front-end keywords appear on the product _____, _____ and _____, while back-end keywords are _____ within a listing.

5. Amazon advertising might be expensive, but it can help you _____, _____ and increase your sales.

6. Off-store marketing refers to the promotional activities through tools and channels _____ Amazon.

Ⅲ. **Translate the following passage into Chinese.**

You can select the best tools to design your very own Amazon marketing strategy. Some experts suggest to loop all the marketing activities into the system, believing the cross-channel marketing campaign is more powerful to achieve business goals.

Module Three Project Implementation

A Step-by-Step Guide to Create a Promotion on Amazon

Amazon promotion is a powerful tool that can help Amazon sellers fulfill a wide range of goals. By running promotions you can boost short-term sales, generate reviews for new products. Here are the steps to create an effective Amazon promotion strategy (Fig. 7-5).

Unit Three Marketing

Fig. 7-5 Create Promotions

Step 1: Create Promotions

Log in to your Seller Central Account and hover over the Advertising menu on the top of the page. From the drop-down menu, choose Promotions (Fig. 7-6).

Fig. 7-6 Amazon Promotions

Step 2: Choose Promotion Ways

On the Promotions page, you will be using the initial Create a Promotion tab which offers Social Media Promo Code, Percentage Off and Buy One Get One. Percentage Off will be chosen here.

7-3 介绍社交媒体
促销代码

Step 3: Set Conditions

Percentage Off page is divided into three sections—Conditions, Scheduling, and Additional Options. You will begin with the first section—Conditions (Fig. 7-7). In the Conditions section, choose the number of items a customer must purchase in order to get the discount from the "At least this quantity of items" drop-down menu. If you simply want to offer a coupon code for a single product, choose "1". For bulk discounts, choose "2" or more.

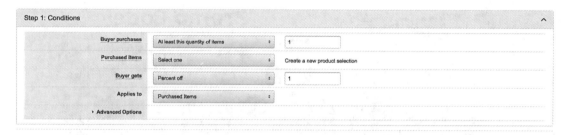

Fig. 7-7 Set Conditions

Now choose "Create a new product selection" at the end of the Purchased Items line. This will allow you to choose which products will be discounted (Fig. 7-8).

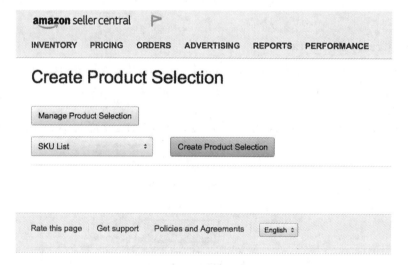

Fig. 7-8 Select a Product

From the drop-down menu, choose "SKU list", then click on Create Product Selection. Now you can begin to tell Amazon which products to discount. On the Create Product Selection page, enter the Product Selection Name or Tracking ID for your product, include an internal description for your own use, then enter the SKU number (or numbers) which are attached to the product you wish to discount. Once you have chosen the SKU, click on Submit (Fig. 7-9).

Once you have submitted the SKU, you will be taken back to the Create a Promotion: Percentage Off page. Now in the Purchased Items drop-down menu you should choose the product you just named. On the Buyer Gets line, choose the percentage discount that you would like to offer. For example, if you wish to offer a 40% discount, insert a value of

Fig. 7-9　Create Product Selection

"40". On the next line, choose "Applies to" Purchased Items. (Note: If you'd like to exclude certain items or offer tiered discounts for multiple products purchased, click on Advanced Options below the "Applies to" line.)

Step 4: Set Scheduling

Let's move on to the second section which is fairly easy—Scheduling (Fig. 7-10). Choose the beginning and ending dates and times of your promotion. (Note: Amazon requires 4 hours to process your promotional code, so you must choose a time at least 4 hours from your current time.) If you'd like to include an Internal Description, you may, but this is completely for your own reference. You do not need to enter a Tracking ID since Amazon provides one for you.

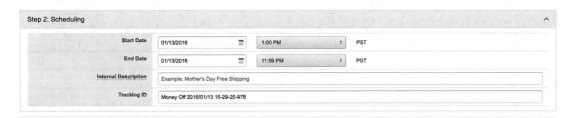

Fig. 7-10　Scheduling

Step 5: Set Additional Options

Section three (Additional Options) is not difficult, but it is where many sellers make a huge mistake and rapidly lose inventory and money. So pay close attention! If you leave the default selection of "None," every individual will receive your product for the discounted price whether they have the coupon/claim code or not. If you select the "Group" option, your promotion will have a single claim code but the code can be used by multiple people. So, in the event that the code is posted online, your entire inventory could sell out very quickly (Fig. 7-11).

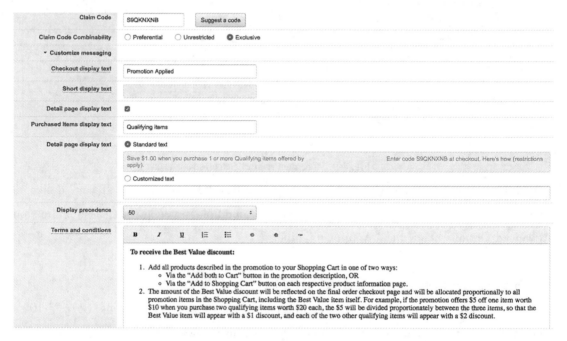

Fig. 7-11　Additional Options SSSeSConditionsRegistration

Once you have clicked on the "Single-use" button, more options will appear. Check the box next to "One redemption per customer" to limit every customer to a single discount. To create a claim code, you can allow Amazon to assign one randomly by clicking on "Suggest a code" or you may create your own. Keep in mind that claim codes can only be 8 characters and only numbers and letters. Once you have created a claim code, it may not be used for another Amazon promotion. Leave Claim Code Combinability at the default "Exclusive" (Fig. 7-12).

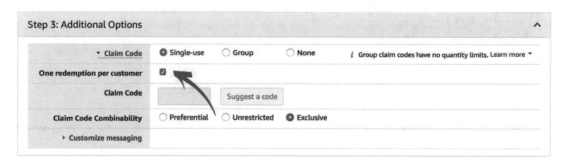

Fig. 7-12　Claim Code

Click on the blue, highlighted Customize Messaging link, and do not forget to UNCHECK the box next to "Detail page display text". If you do not disable this default choice, every customer will be able to see the details of your promotion and coupon code on your listing. At the bottom of the page, click on "Review". This will give you a chance to give a once-over to all the choices you made before you submit the promotion.

Once submit the promotion, remember to allow 4 hours for the code to process. If you'd like to check on the status, from your Seller Central Account choose Advertising then Promotions then Manage Promotions. There you will see whether the promotion is processing or completed (Fig. 7-13). Hopefully, these steps will make setting up a promotional campaign much easier for you.

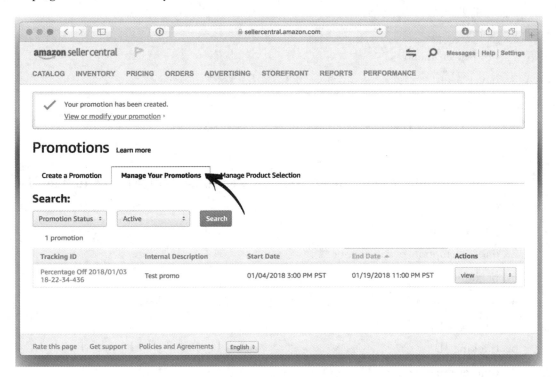

Fig. 7-13　Promotion Management

Exercises

Ⅰ. Match the words or phrases on the left with their Chinese versions on the right.

1. Percentage Off
2. Social Media Promo Code
3. randomly
4. submit
5. coupon
6. status
7. drop-down menu
8. hover over
9. default
10. Buy One Get One

a. 随机地
b. 社交媒体促销代码
c. 买一赠一
d. 提交
e. 购买折扣
f. 下拉菜单
g. 状态
h. 悬停
i. 优惠券
j. 默认的

Ⅱ. Put the information about Amazon Percentage Off Setting in the right category.

1. purchased items
2. one redemption per customer
3. beginning dates
4. product selection name
5. ending dates
6. tracking ID
7. time of promotion
8. create a claim code
9. SKU list
10. customize messaging

Conditions Setting	Scheduling Setting	Additional Options Setting

III. Read the passage carefully and fill in the blanks with the items provided.

A. check the box next to "One redemption per customer"
B. click on "Review"
C. click on Manage Promotions
D. a single product
E. "at least this quantity"
F. "detail page display text"

1. If you need limit every customer to a single discount, you have to _____.
2. If Amazon sellers want to check on the status to see whether the promotion is processing or completed, they have to _____.
3. Amazon sellers can _____ in order to give once-over to all the choices they have made before submitting the promotion.
4. From the _____ drop-down menu, Amazon sellers can choose the number of items a customer must purchase in order to get the discount.
5. If you simply want to offer a coupon code for _____, choose "1". For bulk discounts, choose "2" or more.
6. Every customer will be able to see the details of your promotion and coupon code on your listing if the Amazon sellers fail to uncheck the box next to _____.

Notes for 1+X Certificate

Things to Do before Promoting Your Amazon Products

If you are a new seller looking to boost your ratings and reviews, below are some important things you need to do before promoting your Amazon products.

· **Make your products more competitive**

Advertising is a great way to boost your product sales, and so is selling products that are a little different to other sellers' products. If you are selling the same product as another seller, add a discount, promote your coupons, or sell it in different colors.

· **Amazon SEO**

Ensure that your listing has good Amazon Search Engine Optimization (SEO). This will help potential customers find your products easier using a specific set of keywords.

· **Learn about the Amazon Buy Box**

Study the rules of the Buy Box and win the Buy Box with repricing tools that are easy to find online. The Buy Box is the box that appears on product detail pages where customers add items to their cart. It is competitive, and the only way to win it is to have competitive pricing and offers in your store with a great Amazon merchant history.

You will need to be an amazing seller to covet one of the Buy Box positions available.

Task 8　Amazon Advertising

 Project Description

As an advertising campaign planner working for Amazon business, you are going to make full use of Amazon promotional tools and Amazon Advertising to improve sales and boost visibility.

 Project Requirement

· Launch Amazon Advertising campaigns to boost sales and visibility.

 Learning Goals

· Acquire basic knowledge about platform-inside marketing tools of Amazon.
· Master the procedure of creating and managing promotional activities and campaigns inside Amazon.
· Master words and expressions related to Amazon advertising.

Module One　Warm-up

Marketing activities are important to Amazon sellers. Please work with your partners to find out ways of product promotion appearing in the picture.

 ## Module Two　Reading

Ways to Promote Your Products on Amazon Site

When you start selling your products on Amazon, there are numerous ways that can help your products sell fast and increase your sales. Amazon features many in-house advertising tools for marketing activities. Below are some practical ways that will help you figure out how to promote Amazon products inside Amazon.

1. Amazon Lightning Deals

Amazon Lightning Deals are promotional offers that only last for a short period of time (Fig. 8-1). The best thing about lightning deals is that there is a dedicated page on Amazon for them, where they can be listed as long as the discount is at least 30% more than the original price of your product.

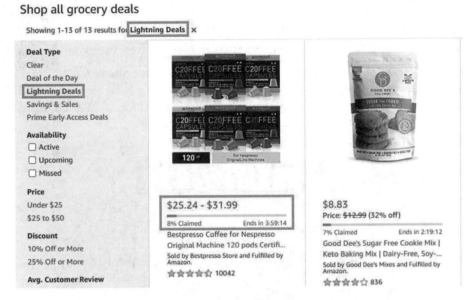

Fig. 8-1 Lightning Deals

2. Amazon Discounts

Discounts can tempt your customers into buying more than they usually would. Discounts are one of the most basic ways to know how to promote Amazon products without putting in too much effort.

3. Amazon Promotions

Amazon promotion sellers can offer their products at a low cost. Since Amazon audiences love a good deal, using Amazon Promotions is a great opportunity for you to grab their attention (Fig. 8-2).

Fig. 8-2 Promotion Activities

4. Amazon Prime

Amazon features more than 100 million Amazon Prime members, and they all love to use their Amazon Prime benefits, including free two-day shipping. On Amazon, users can even filter products to exclude items not eligible for Amazon Prime (Fig. 8-3).

8-1 介绍亚马逊 Prime 会员福利

Fig. 8-3 Prime Day

5. Amazon Advertising

Advertising on Amazon is an effective way to drive traffic and sales of listed products. It also can be a great tool to boost brand or product awareness and visibility as Amazon sponsored ads often appear at the top of search result pages.

There are 3 types of sponsored ads (Fig. 8-4).

(1) Sponsored Products are cost-per-click (CPC) ads that promote individual product listings on Amazon. They appear within shopping results pages and on product detail pages. Sponsored Products can help you reach high-intent shoppers who are actively looking for products related to theirs.

(2) Sponsored Brands are cost-per-click (CPC) ads that feature your brand logo, a custom headline, and multiple products. These ads appear in shopping results helping drive sales and product visibility. Sponsored Brands give you the opportunity to quickly grow consideration for your brand and collection of products from shoppers who have expressed an interest in similar products.

(3) Sponsored Display is a new self-service advertising solution that helps advertisers reach relevant audiences across the shopper journey. These ads appear on and off Amazon which help you reach the right audience for your business.

Unit Three　Marketing

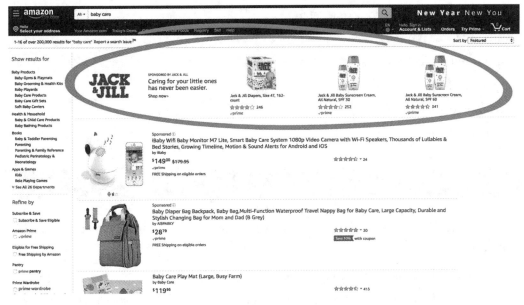

Fig. 8-4　Sponsored Display

New Words and Expressions

numerous /ˈnjuːmərəs/ adj. 很多的;众多的;许多的

dedicated /ˈdedɪkeɪtɪd/ adj. 献身的;专用的;专心致志的

tempt /tempt/ v. 引诱;诱惑

essential /ɪˈsenʃl/ adj. 本质的;必不可少的;极其重要的

exclude /ɪkˈskluːd/ v. 排除(……的可能性);不包括

eligible /ˈelɪdʒəbl/ adj. 有资格的;合格的

drive traffic 吸引流量

high-intent 有强烈意向的

self-service 自助式

a good deal 便宜商品

Terms

brand logo　品牌标志

Amazon Lightning Deals　亚马逊秒杀活动

Amazon Discounts　亚马逊打折活动

Amazon Promotion   亚马逊促销活动
Amazon Prime   亚马逊 Prime 会员
CPC ads   点击付费广告
sponsored ads   赞助广告
Sponsored Products   商品推广
Sponsored Brands   品牌推广
Sponsored Display   展示型推广

Exercises

Ⅰ. **Write T for true or F for false in the brackets beside the following statements about the text.**

1. Amazon does not provide any advertising tools for its sellers.　　　　(　　)
2. Amazon Promotions is a great opportunity for Amazon sellers to grab the buyers' attention.　　　　(　　)
3. It is estimated that there are more than 1000 million Amazon Prime members.　　　　(　　)
4. Amazon Prime benefits do not include free two-day shipping.　　　　(　　)
5. There are 4 types of Amazon sponsored ads including Sponsored Products, Sponsored Brands, Sponsored Display and Stores.　　　　(　　)
6. Amazon Advertising is a powerful way to increase traffic and sales of listed products.　　　　(　　)
7. Sponsored Products only appears on shopping results pages.　　　　(　　)
8. Sponsored Brands features the Amazon sellers' brand logo, a custom headline, and multiple products.　　　　(　　)
9. Sponsored Display helps the advertiser reach the right audience for their business.　　　　(　　)
10. All the Amazon sponsored ads are free.　　　　(　　)

Ⅱ. **Read the text again and fill in the blanks in the following sentences.**

1. Amazon Prime members all love to use their Amazon Prime benefits, including _____ _____.
2. Amazon Advertising is an effective way to drive _____ and _____ of listed products.

3. Amazon Advertising is a great tool to boost visibility because Amazon sponsored ads often appear _____.
4. There are 3 types of Amazon sponsored ads including _____, _____ and _____.
5. Sponsored Products are cost-per-click (CPC) ads that promote individual product listings on Amazon, which appear within _____ and on _____.
6. Sponsored Brands are cost-per-click (CPC) ads that feature the _____, _____ and _____.

III. Translate the following passage into Chinese.

Amazon features more than 100 million Amazon Prime members, and they all love to use their Amazon Prime benefits, including free two-day shipping. On Amazon, users can even filter products to exclude items not eligible for Amazon Prime.

Module Three Project Implementation

A Step by Step Guide:
Create the Sponsored Products Campaign on Amazon

As the most common and effective type of Amazon pay-per-click (PPC) ads, Sponsored Product Ads are used by 66% of Amazon sellers (Fig. 8-5). Since they can help customers find products quickly in related shopping results and products pages, sponsored products campaigns are extremely valuable to sellers by boosting visibility and increasing sales. For Amazon beginners, it is highly recommended to start with the Sponsored Products campaign with automatic targeting. You can easily set up your campaign by following these simple steps.

8-2 如何优化自动投放型商品推广活动

Step 1: Log in to your Seller Central account.

On the homepage, click on "Advertising" tab. Choose Campaign Manager from the "Advertising" menu.

Fig. 8-5 Amazon Sponsored Products

Step 2: Create Campaign.

From the Campaign Manager page (Fig. 8-6), Click on "Create campaign" (Fig. 8-7).

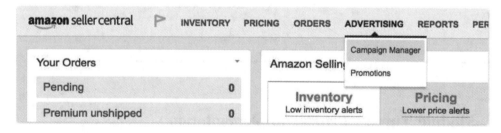

Fig. 8-6 Campaign Manager

Fig. 8-7 Create Campaign

Step 3: Choose the Campaign Type.

After you click on the "Create campaign" button then select Sponsored Products (Fig. 8-8).

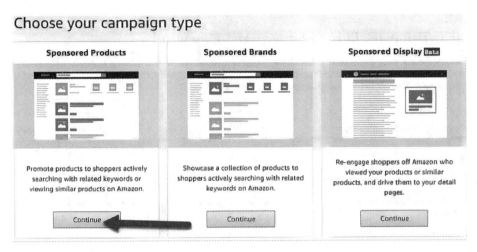

Fig. 8-8 Campaign Type

Step 4: Create the Settings for Your Campaign.

Once you have picked your sponsored products, you can set the following parameters (Fig. 8-9).

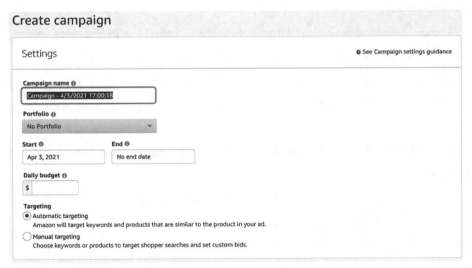

Fig. 8-9 Create the Settings

(1) Campaign name: Give a name so later you can find it easily.

(2) Daily budget: Put an amount of budget you want to spend daily.

(3) Duration: You can put an end date if you want to stop the campaign after a fixed time. Otherwise you can skip it.

(4) Targeting: Select automatic targeting.

Step 5: Define the Bidding Strategy and Placement.

Now you can set campaign bidding strategy and placement. Amazon offers 3 types of bidding strategy and 2 types of placement (Fig. 8-10).

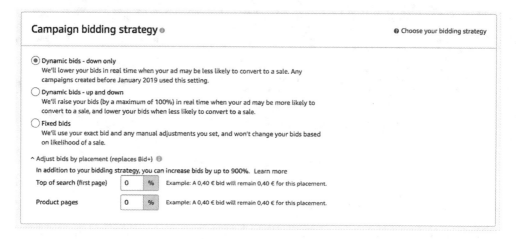

Fig. 8-10　Define Bidding Strategy

Bidding Strategy

(1) Dynamic bids down only: Amazon will lower your bids in real-time when your ad may be less likely to convert a sale.

(2) Dynamic bids up and down: Amazon will raise your bids in real-time when your ad may be more likely to convert to a sale, and lower your bids when less likely to convert a sale.

(3) Fixed bids: Amazon will use your exact bid and any manual adjustment you set.

Placement

(1) Top of search: You can set a percentage that Amazon can increase in real-time to show your product in the top search.

(2) Product pages: You can set a percentage that Amazon can increase in real-time to show your product under product pages.

Step 6: Create an Ad Group for Your Products.

In this section, you create an ad group and then choose the products you want to advertise. To do so, select the products you want to advertise in this ad group. You can search and add or you can enter the ASINs to add. Also Amazon offers bulk upload to add items (Fig. 8-11).

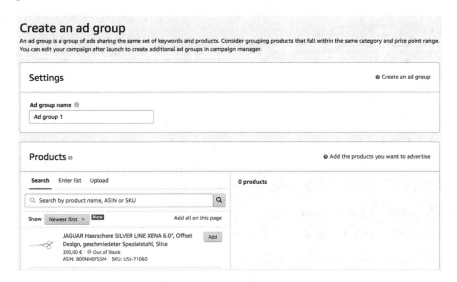

Fig. 8-11 Create an Ad Group

Step 7: Set CPC Bidding.

Now it is time to bid. Amazon does suggest a bid to start and also they put it as a default bid. Automatic campaigns offer 4 match types. You can set a default bid for all 4 or separate for each one. We highly recommend using it separately for each one (Fig. 8-12).

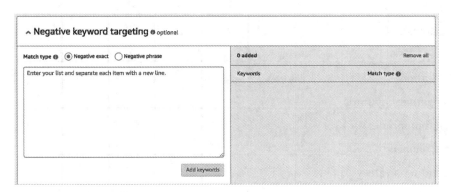

Fig. 8-12 Set CPC Bidding

Step 8: Add Negative Keywords.

Finally, you can put some negative keywords right before starting your campaigns. To avoid unnecessary costs, Amazon offers the sellers the option of excluding inappropriate search terms by adding negative keywords (Fig. 8-13).

Fig. 8-13　Add Negative Keywords

Step 9：Launch Your Campaign.

Click on the Launch Campaign and your first campaign is ready!

Exercises

Ⅰ. Match the words or phrases on the left with their Chinese versions on the right.

1. bulk upload   a. 预算
2. automatic   b. 动态的
3. skip   c. 点击付费广告
4. duration   d. 手动的
5. negative keywords   e. 发布投放
6. inappropriate   f. 推荐
7. recommend   g. 自动的
8. bidding strategy   h. 参数
9. launch   i. 竞价策略
10. budget   j. 否定关键词
11. manual   k. 批量上传
12. dynamic   l. 跳过
13. PPC ads   m. 不恰当的
14. parameter   n. 持续时间

II. Answer the following questions based on the text.

1. Why are sponsored products campaigns important for Amazon sellers?

   _____

2. What will Amazon do when you click on "Dynamic bids up and down" option?

   _____

3. In what ways do Amazon sellers pick advertising products in the ad group?

   _____

4. What is the purpose of adding negative keywords when you are setting Amazon sponsored products campaigns?

   _____

III. Read the text carefully, and fill in the blanks in the table.

A	B
Step_____	Create an ad group and select the _____ you want to advertise in this ad group.
Step_____	Set campaign name, _____, _____ and targeting for your campaign.
Step_____	Set the CPC bidding.
Step_____	Log in your Seller Central account, click on_____tab and choose_____.
Step_____	Set campaign bidding strategy among "dynamic bids down only", "dynamic bids down only" and _____. Set placement between _____ and "product pages".
Step_____	Click on the "Launch Campaign" to complete it.
Step_____	Select_____to define the campaign type.
Step_____	Exclude inappropriate search terms by adding _____.
Step_____	Click on "Create campaign" to start your journey.

Notes for 1+X Certificate

What can Advertising on Amazon Do for Your Brand?

Millions of shoppers are searching for products on Amazon. In fact, nearly 80% of Amazon shoppers use Amazon to discover new products and brands.

Advertising can help customers notice your brand, no matter what stage they are in the decision journey. By appearing in high-impact placements on desktop and mobile devices, advertising helps you maximize exposure on Amazon and reach an engaged audience. Advertising your brand on Amazon, especially with Sponsored Brands, can achieve below.

· Establish brand discovery

Sponsored Brands give you the opportunity to quickly grow consideration for your brand and collection of products with customers who have expressed an interest in products like yours.

· Establish brand measurement

Sponsored Brands use unique metrics like "new-to-brand" so you can measure how many new customers you have gained in the past 12 months and optimize for greater lifetime value.

· Create customer trust

When you link your Sponsored Brands campaign to a store, you extend your interaction past the click. This creates opportunities for deeper connection with potential customers. This connection also allows you to build brand loyalty and provides a chance for up-selling, basket building and bundling.

Task 9　Marketing outside Amazon Platform

 Project Description

As an advertising campaign planner in Amazon business, you are going to launch your marketing activities through other platforms besides Amazon to drive more traffic and sales.

 Project Requirement

· Launch marketing campaigns outside Amazon platform.

 Learning Goals

· Acquire basic knowledge about marketing outside Amazon.
· Master the procedure of promoting Amazon stores and products on other platforms.
· Master words and expressions related to marketing outside Amazon platform.

Module One　Warm-up

If you were an Amazon seller, list at least 3 social platforms that you think will help promote your Amazon products and write down your reasons.

Social platform	Reason

 Module Two　Reading

How to Promote Amazon Products Offsite to Grow Your Business

Advertising your products outside of Amazon is vital to boost your sales, and will help promote your Amazon store, too. To be a successful Amazon seller, you should be aware of the following offsite marketing strategies.

· **Work with influencers**

Amazon listings can gain valuable traffic through influencer marketing (Fig. 9-1). When prominent and credible individuals within your industry stand behind your product and share a link to your listing, it signals that your product is worth checking out. You can easily reach out to influencers who exist on every channel from YouTube to Instagram to promote your Amazon products for you.

· **Promote on social platform**

Sharing your Amazon listings on social media, such as Facebook, Instagram, or TikTok, is a powerful way of getting your products in front of more potential buyers (Fig. 9-2). Your social media followers expect to see value in your posts, so avoid creating pure-ad posts. Instead, share your listing in a more subtle way.

Fig. 9-1　Influencer Marketing

Fig. 9-2　Social Media Marketing

· **Drive traffic from blogs**

Discover blogs that write about your products and ask them to partner with you to promote your products. Similarly to working with influencers, reputable blog writers will know how to promote Amazon products in the best way.

· **Social ads**

By making use of ad services on social websites, like Facebook ads, Google search ads and other paid channels, you will be able to push more traffic towards your product listings (Fig. 9-3). This works similarly to Amazon Pay Per Click (PPC) ads, and it can also be effective when you use product landing pages.

> The easiest way to shave - your blades just arrive in the mail once a month and you don't have to worry about ordering them. The blades are cheaper than the big-name supermarket blades too.
>
> RD.SHAVED.BY
> **Get Ready with a Starter Set!**
> There's no better way to experience a delicious sampling of what DSC has...
>
> 👍 Like   💬 Comment   ↗ Share   🗂 Buffer

Fig. 9-3 Ad on Twitter

· **Deals sites**

Deals websites like Slickdeals are great for promoting your products (Fig. 9-4). If your product becomes popular enough for the front page of any deals websites, you will be able to achieve more organic traffic, leading to more sales. When you are struggling to figure out how to promote Amazon products, deals websites are good for a first point-of-call.

9-1 Slickdeals
论坛发布规则

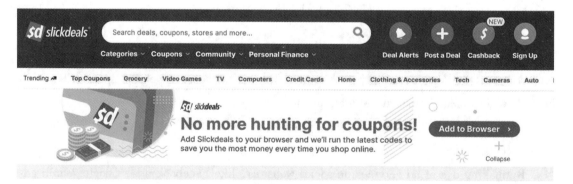

Fig. 9-4 Deals Website

· **Offer coupons**

If you happen to have a large list of subscribers (on YouTube, social media etc.), you can easily distribute coupons to them (Fig. 9-5). People enjoy discounted items. We all look for a great deal, so offering coupons to individuals who have already provided their information to you is a natural business step to take.

Fig. 9-5　Coupons

New Words and Expressions

prominent /ˈprɒmɪnənt/ *adj.* 重要的；著名的
credible /ˈkredəbl/ *adj.* 可信的；可靠的
follower /ˈfɒləʊə(r)/ *n.* 跟随者；粉丝
signal /ˈsɪgnəl/ *v.* 表明；预示；表达；表示；显示
reputable /ˈrepjətəbl/ *adj.* 有信誉的；声誉好的
potential /pəˈtenʃl/ *adj.* 潜在的；可能的
coupon /ˈkuːpɒn/ *n.* （购物）优惠券
blog /blɒg/ *n.* 博客
subscriber /səbˈskraɪbə(r)/ *n.* （报刊的）订阅人；订购人
first point-of-call 首要措施
check out 结账；买单
reach out 伸出手；联系
social platform 社交平台

Terms

offsite marketing strategy　站外营销策略
Google search ads　谷歌搜索广告
landing page　登录页
deals site　折扣网站
organic traffic　自然流量
Slickdeals　简称SD,目前美国最大、最具影响力的折扣信息分享交流平台
Facebook　脸书（社交网站）
TikTok　抖音（社交网站）
YouTube　油管（社交网站）
Instagram　照片墙（社交网站）

Exercises

Ⅰ. Write T for true or F for false in the brackets beside the following statements about the text.

1. To achieve success in Amazon business, it is very important to market your products outside Amazon. （　）
2. Influencer marketing can help drive traffic to the Amazon listings. （　）
3. It is very difficult to contact influencers in Amazon advertising campaign. （　）
4. Influencers only exist on YouTube. （　）
5. It is not wise to post pure ads on your social platforms, because your followers tend to seek valuable information on your posts. （　）
6. Influential blog writers will know how to promote Amazon products in the best way. （　）
7. Facebook ads, Google search ads and other paid channels do not work in the same way as Amazon PPC ads. （　）
8. Slickdeals is a very popular social platform. （　）
9. You must daily distribute coupons on the social platforms. （　）
10. It is a fact that people like discounted products. （　）

II. **Read the text again and fill in the blanks in the following sentences.**

1. Advertising your products outside of Amazon is essential to _____ and _____, too.
2. Your social media followers expect to see value in your posts, so avoid creating pure-ad posts. Instead, share your listing in a more _____ way.
3. To drive traffic from the blog, you need to discover the blogs that write about _____ and ask them to partner with you.
4. If your product becomes popular on front page of deals websites, you will be able to achieve more _____, which will naturally lead to more _____.
5. When you are struggling to figure out how to promote Amazon products, _____ are good for a first point-of-call.
6. People all look for a great deal, so it is a natural business step to take to _____ to individuals.

III. **Translate the following passage into Chinese.**

If you happen to have a large list of subscribers (on YouTube, social media etc.), you can easily distribute coupons to them. People enjoy discounted items. We all look for a great deal, so offering coupons to individuals who have already provided their information to you is a natural business step to take.

Module Three Project Implementation

How to Market Your Amazon Products on Facebook Groups

Facebook group is an online community for almost every hobby you could think of. More than 1.8 billion Facebook users are active in groups at least once a month and it is a fun platform where you can communicate directly with your readers.

What's more, if you are an Amazon business owner, a Facebook group that is owned by someone else can be a great marketing tool. A successful Facebook group can help Amazon sellers drive more traffic, turn casual website visitors into loyal customers, promote products within the group to boost sales and collect feedback about products. There are millions of Facebook groups so there is a good chance that there is already a group around your topic.

9-2 Facebook 营销技巧

You can simply follow three steps to join the existing communities and begin connecting with potential customers to promote your business.

Step 1: Log in

Go to the Facebook website and log in to your account (Fig. 9-6).

Fig. 9-6 Log in

Step 2: Identify Your Target Groups

Click the search box on the top of the Facebook page and enter a keyword or set of keywords that best describes the type of group you wish to join (Fig. 9-7). For instance, if your business sells clothes for pets, you can try searching for "Pet lovers" or any related group with pet owners as they are most likely to find your business interesting. Click the See More Results link on the bottom of the box that appears below the search box. Click

Unit Three　Marketing

"Groups" under the Search Filters portion of the left sidebar. Click on the group from the list of results to see more details about the group (Fig. 9-8).

Fig. 9-7　Enter Keywords

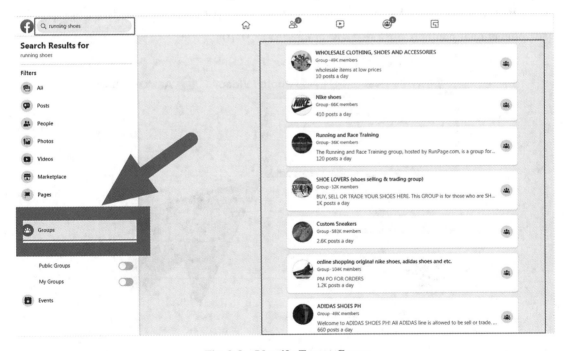

Fig. 9-8　Identify Target Group

Step 3: Join Groups

Click the Join Group button to join the group so you can promote your business (Fig. 9-9). If the group is an Open Group you can post immediately after joining. Otherwise, you will have to wait for a group administrator to accept you.

Fig. 9-9　Join Group

Once you have found your Facebook groups, here are some tips for you when posting your promotional contents on Facebook groups (Fig. 9-10).

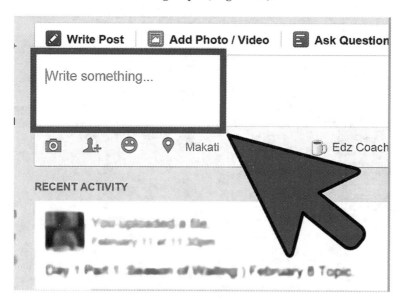

Fig. 9-10　Write Post

(1) Read the rules of each group you join and respect them! Breaking rules will not only get you kicked out of a group but it could lead to a bad reputation among your community.

(2) Take some time to get to know the lay of the land and the tone of the group before you decide on the types of content you want to write.

(3) Engaging with content in the group to build awareness on Facebook is important. Creating content related to current affairs is a great way of boosting your business and at the same time make sure that you have active participation in your group.

(4) Provide value and not go for the straightforward sale. Your reader wants information that is relevant to their interests, more than that, they want information that is educational and interesting. So it is important to ask questions, be friendly, answer questions helpfully and share valuable insights on the groups.

(5) Always remember to add a tint of humour to your posts. Humorous content will always have a place in marketing and advertising. When you do it right, it can attract attention as well as <u>compel</u> the audience to know more about your business and services.

If you are promoting Amazon products to your group, explain why you are posting the link or promotion, because nobody joins a group to be spammed to death with links and sales messages.

Exercises

I. Match the words or phrases on the left with their Chinese versions on the right.

1. compel
2. group administrator
3. spam
4. feedback
5. straightforward
6. Facebook Group
7. community
8. participation
9. insight
10. casual
11. a tint of
12. Search Filters
13. tone
14. target groups

a. 社区
b. 参与
c. 反馈
d. 直接的
e. 迫使
f. 目标群组
g. 见解
h. 脸书群组
i. 搜索筛选器
j. 随意的
k. 一层……色彩
l. 群管理员
m. 向……发送垃圾信息
n. 风格，特色

II. **Read the text carefully, and choose the right answer to each question.**

1. Which of the following statement is not true based on this text? ( )

    A. Facebook group is a fun community where people can communicate.

    B. Facebook group can be a great marketing tool for Amazon sellers.

    C. Facebook group has more than 1.8 million active users.

    D. Facebook group is for almost every hobby you could think of.

2. What are the potential benefits brought by Facebook group marketing to Amazon sellers? ( )

    A. Drive more traffic and collect feedback about products.

    B. Turn casual website visitors into loyal customers.

    C. Promote products within the group to boost sales.

    D. All of the above.

3. In order to identify your target groups, you need to _____. ( )

    A. explain why you are posting the link or promotion

    B. click the search box and enter the keywords that best describes the type of group you hope to join

    C. ask questions friendly

    D. ask your audience to know more about your business and services

4. The underlined word "compel" in this text means_____. ( )

    A. attract

    B. require

    C. prevent

    D. order

5. When you start posting your promotional contents on Facebook groups, you have to _____. ( )

    A. provide information that is directly related to your business and services

    B. avoid answering questions and sharing insights on the groups

    C. respect the rules of each group

    D. write serious and formal contents

III. **Look at the following post, do you think the promotional content is successful? Please give your reasons.**

Hello, my name is Jon Morrow

The first thing you should know about me is I have voice-activated shotguns embedded in

my wheelchair, and I'm not afraid to use them.

Okay, not really, but I'm almost that cool.

You see, I have a type of muscular dystrophy called SMA, and over the years, it slowly stolen my ability to move anything but my face. I'm writing to you now with a microphone and speech recognition software called Dragon Naturally Speaking.

Aside: You can watch an entire video about the speech recognition stuff here. Just be aware that the sweater makes me look fatter than I actually am.

But the really cool part?

I live in West Palm Beach.

 Notes for 1+X Certificate

Tips on How to Sell Amazon Products on Instagram

Social media is a powerful tool to advertise your Amazon products, and Instagram is a prime choice for most sellers because it has the highest engagement rate compared to any other social media platform. Here are some tips when advertising your Amazon products on Instagram in order to drive more traffic and increase sales.

(1) Hire a professional photographer to take product images as they will know how to get the lighting, angles, and aesthetics right.

(2) Use catchy, witty, or sometimes even funny captions for your posts. A good sense of humor can go a long way in capturing the attention of your audience.

(3) Whatever posts you are putting up on Instagram, be as consistent as you can and post regularly. This will help you gain attraction. Posting irregularly will lead to your audience losing interest, so keep them engaged with regular posts.

(4) Keep your account open to the public. Having a private account is only going to cut down your audience reach. Not everyone is willing to send a request and wait for you to accept. It is just easier for the audience to be able to follow, view and like your posts when your account is open. Your posts may even be displayed for people who do not follow you, thus enabling you to spread your brand message more effectively.

(5) Do not forget to provide links in your Instagram posts to your Amazon products so that interested buyers can easily visit your listing and make a purchase.

(6) Collaborate with other brands. You can ask similar brands to promote your products in exchange for you doing the same for them. This way you can effectively reach a wider audience and enhance the visibility of your brand.

(7) Work with influencers on Instagram who have a huge follower base. If sellers want to give their listings a powerful boost in terms of traffic and sales, influencer marketing can be highly beneficial. When influencers post the products on Instagram, their followers are guaranteed to check out what the products are about and buy them.

Supplementary Reading

9-3 直播

Unit Four

Customer Service

Task 10   Customer Questions

 Project Description

To provide positive customer experience and finally convert customers into loyal fans of your brand, you will need to answer your customer questions properly on the listing or through the buyer-seller messages.

 Project Requirement

· Communicate with customers on the listing or through the buyer-seller messages.

 Learning Goals

· Understand the importance of answering customer questions on the listing or through buyer-seller messages.

· Master the procedures to answer customer questions on the listing or through the buyer-seller messages and know the best practices when communicating with customers.

· Master words and expressions related to customer questions.

Unit Four　Customer Service

 Module One　Warm-up

Look at the following picture, please ask more questions about the product as a buyer.

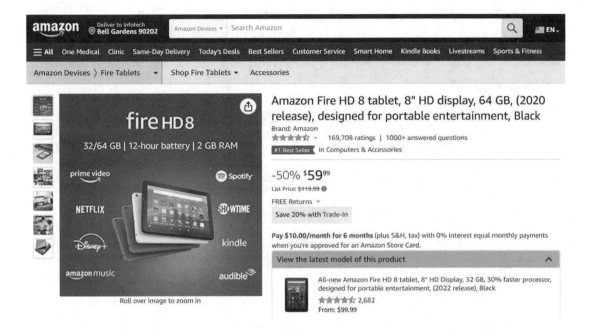

Customer questions & answers

	Question:	Is youtube on this device ?
0 votes	Answer:	No the official YouTube app is not in the Amazon App Store. By Jackie Elin on January 31, 2023
		˅ See more answers (2)

	Question:	Can I check my email with this tablet?
0 votes	Answer:	There's an email app that comes with the Fire, but I haven't tried that. However, if you use AOL for email (e.g., via Verizon), you can download the AOL app that gives you access to all your accounts. By MikeC on February 21, 2023
		˅ See more answers (4)

Module Two Reading

How to Answer Amazon Customer Questions

10-1 什么是顾客保留及顾客保留的益处

Customer service is an integral part of successful business, especially on Amazon. A positive customer experience not only helps with customer retention but increases your chances of receiving positive feedback and reviews (Fig. 10-1, Fig. 10-2, Fig. 10-3).

Fig. 10-1 Questions on the Listing

From the United States

Lynn Campbell VINE VOICE

★☆☆☆☆ Won't Hold Up
Reviewed in the United States on January 2, 2023
Size: 7.5ft   Color: Red   Verified Purchase
I ordered this bag to store a slim pencil tree, 7 ft tall. It arrived Dec 10, 2022 so this is the first use, packing away Christmas this year. I opened the bag, laid the tree parts inside and when I began zipping it closed, I saw several inches of the stitching along the top was not caught. The zipper is fine but the stitching that runs parallel to the zipper was not caught in the sewing of the bag, so it's gaping open for several inches and any slight movement of the bag will cause the stitching to further come apart. Don't waste your money on this tree storage bag. The quality is lacking.

Fig. 10-2 Negative Review

Fig. 10-3 Feedback

The last thing you want is for a customer to leave negative feedback about their experience with your business. Seller feedback impacts your overall account health and rating, so it is important that you take measures to keep it positive.

If you use FBA, Amazon will handle most of the customer service for you, though there may be some instances where you will need to interact with the customer directly.

In this article, we will go over the customer interactions you may encounter as an Amazon seller, along with our best practices for converting customers into loyal fans of your brand.

· **Answering questions on your listing**

On Amazon, customers are able to ask questions about your product directly on your listing. Once the questions are answered, they will be publicly visible on your listing page, just above the customer review section.

Both the seller and other customers can answer these questions. Once a customer asks a question, customers who have purchased that product in the past may receive an email of the question with an option to answer. You as the seller will also receive an email notifying you of the question.

Amazon labels questions answered by the seller or manufacturer (Fig. 10-4), so shoppers know it came straight from the source.

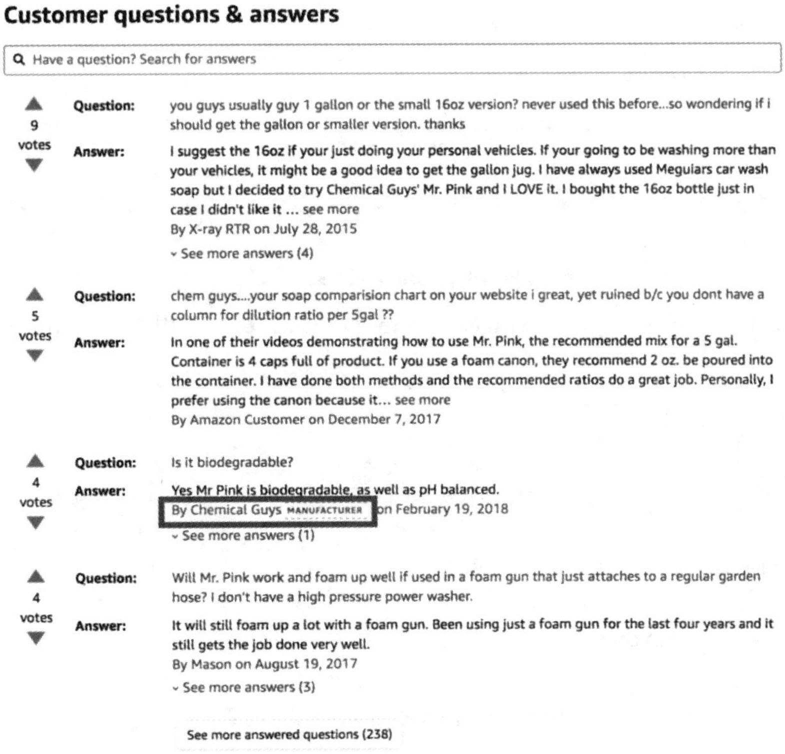

Fig. 10-4　Answer from Manufacturer

· **Buyer-seller messages**

Amazon has strict communication guidelines when it comes to contacting their customers, though customers are still able to reach out to you if they have any questions or issues.

Note: You can no longer leave a comment on your product reviews. In the past, sellers could respond to negative reviews with a public comment to remediate the situation. Now, your best bet for addressing and preventing negative feedback is by answering customer questions instead.

If you receive a message from a customer, it will show up within your Seller Central account (Fig. 10-5).

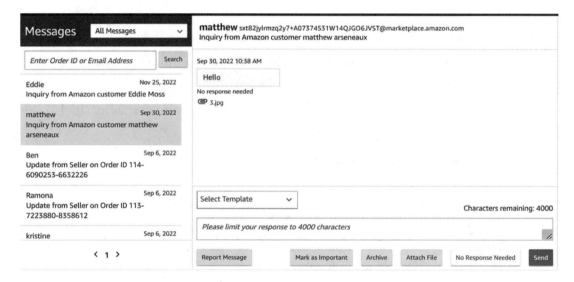

Fig. 10-5 Buyer Messages

You must respond to these messages within 24 hours or it will hurt your account health rating (Fig. 10-6).

Buyer messages ···

	Under 24 hour target	Over 24 hour target
^ **North America**	**0**	**0**
United States: Amazon.com	0	0

Fig. 10-6 Buyer Messages Health Rating

Once in a while, you may receive some spam messages here, but you will still need to take action on them. If it is spam, or you feel you do not need to answer the message, you can mark it as No Response Needed.

· **Best practices**

Best practices when communicating with customers include answering listing questions as quickly as possible, being informative, personalizing your answers, answering account messages within 24 hours, offering the best solution for the customer, not blaming the customer and so on.

A positive customer experience equals more positive feedback and reviews for your Amazon business.

New Words and Expressions

integral /ˈɪntɪgrəl/ adj. 完整的;不可或缺的
retention /rɪˈtenʃn/ n. 保持;维持
impact /ˈɪmpækt/ v. (对某事物)有影响
handle /ˈhændl/ v. 处理,应付
instance /ˈɪnstəns/ n. 实例
interact /ˌɪntərˈækt/ v. 交流
encounter /ɪnˈkaʊntə(r)/ n. 遭遇;遇到
convert /kənˈvɜːt/ v. 转变;转化
visible /ˈvɪzəbl/ adj. 看得见的;可见的
purchase /ˈpɜːtʃəs/ v. 购买
option /ˈɒpʃn/ n. 选择权
notify /ˈnəʊtɪfaɪ/ v. 通知
manufacturer /ˌmænjuˈfæktʃərə(r)/ n. 制造商
source /sɔːs/ n. 信息来源
guideline /ˈgaɪdlaɪn/ n. 准则
remediate /rɪˈmiːdieɪt/ v. 补救
address /əˈdres/ v. 设法解决
equal /ˈiːkwəl/ v. 比得上,敌得过
the last thing 最不愿意做的事情

go over 认真讨论;用心思考
reach out to 联系

Terms

customer retention　客户保留
seller feedback　卖家反馈
account health rating　账户健康评级
spam messages　垃圾邮件

Exercises

Ⅰ. Write T for true or F for false in the brackets beside the following statements about the text.

1. If you want to be a successful seller on Amazon, customer service is essential. 　　　　　　　　　　　　　　　　　　　　　　　　　　　　　　　　　　(　)
2. A positive customer experience is helpful for maintaining customers and getting positive feedback and reviews.　　　　　　　　　　　　　　　　　(　)
3. It is not a big deal if your customer leave negative feedback about your business.　　　　　　　　　　　　　　　　　　　　　　　　　　　　(　)
4. Whether you use FBA or not, you will need to communicate with customer directly.　　　　　　　　　　　　　　　　　　　　　　　　　　　(　)
5. Every customer can see the questions and answers on your listing page. (　)
6. Only seller, manufacturer and customers who bought the product have the right to answer the questions on the listing of that product.　　　　　　(　)
7. Shoppers do not know if the question on the listing is answered by a seller or a buyer.　　　　　　　　　　　　　　　　　　　　　　　　　　(　)
8. Customers cannot contact the seller because of Amazon's strict communication guidelines.　　　　　　　　　　　　　　　　　　　　　　　　　(　)
9. A seller can leave a comment on customer's negative review.　　　(　)
10. Your account health rating will not be affected if you answer a message from a customer beyond 24 hours.　　　　　　　　　　　　　　　　　(　)

II. Read the text again and fill in the blanks in the following sentences.

1. Because _____ has an effect on the overall account health and rating, it is vital for you to take measures to _____.
2. Customers on Amazon can see the questions and answers on the listing page, above _____.
3. Currently, a seller can _____ to deal with negative feedback and keep it from happening.
4. In your _____, you can find the messages from your customers.
5. If you do not have to answer a message, you can mark it as _____.
6. To communicate with customers successfully, you can answer listing questions as quickly as possible, _____, _____, answer account messages within 24 hours, _____, and _____.

III. Translate the following passage into Chinese.

The last thing you want is for a customer to leave negative feedback about their experience with your business. Seller feedback impacts your overall account health and rating, so it is important that you take measures to keep it positive.

Module Three　Project Implementation

Contact Buyers via Buyer-seller Messaging

The Buyer-Seller Messaging Center is one of the best Amazon seller resources because it allows you to stay in constant contact with buyers. Buyer-seller communication allows you to receive feedback, offer returns, and get valuable insights from your customers. Remember, a

10-2　在哪些情况下卖家不能联系买家

clear line of communication also helps build trust with customers. Trust is the difference-maker in turning one-time customers into long-term brand ambassadors!

· **Enable buyer-seller messaging**

Buyers can send you messages about your products to your Merchant Default Contact. If you want to change the email address, you will need to do as below.

(1) On the Settings menu, select Notification Preferences (Fig. 10-7).

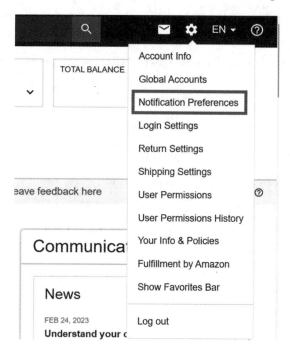

Fig. 10-7　Notification Preferences

(2) In the Messaging section, select Edit (Fig. 10-8).

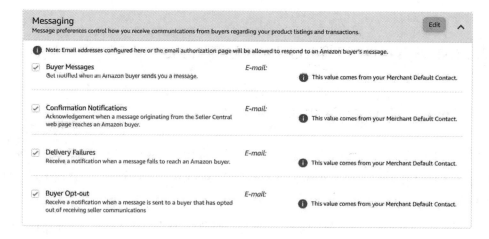

Fig. 10-8　Messaging Setting

(3) Select the Buyer Messages check box, and enter the email address that you want Amazon buyers to send messages to about your products.

(4) Select Save.

· **Contact buyers**

For sellers in the United States, contacting a buyer requires a few steps.

(1) Navigate to the Orders tab and select Manage Orders (Fig. 10-9).

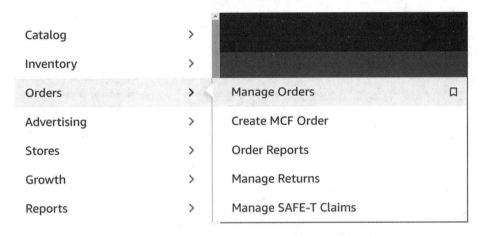

Fig. 10-9 Orders Tab

(2) Find the order that you want to reach out about.

(3) Click on buyer's name to open a new message (Fig. 10-10).

Fig. 10-10 Order Details

(4) Select a "contact reason" on the next page within your seller platform or copy the buyer's encrypted email address from the "To" field and use it within your personal email platform (Fig. 10-11).

Regardless of how you contact buyers, you will not be able to see their real email addresses. Emails will still pass through Amazon's messaging service and appear in buyers' inboxes with your business name in the Sender field.

Contact Buyer

< Back to Manage Orders   Help

Send message to Jeanette

1. Select contact reason

○ Confirm order details Ask your customer a specific order-related question prior to shipping their order.	○ Coordinate large or heavy item shipping Contact your customer to arrange delivery of the order or confirm contact details needed to complete delivery.	○ Send invoice Send the customer an invoice for the order.
○ Courtesy refund Offer a full, courtesy refund or replacement item.	○ Notify of a problem with shipping your order Notify your customer there was an unexpected problem with shipping their order.	○ Other Ask your customer for clarification for a topic not covered by another contact reason.

Fig. 10-11　Contact Reason

You can also send attachments under 10 MB to buyers. Click the paperclip icon within Seller Central to add an attachment to a message or follow the standard attachment process within your email platform if using email.

Now that you know how to contact buyers on Amazon, you can improve customer communications and increase your odds of succeeding as an Amazon seller.

Exercises

I. Translate the following phrases.

1. stay in constant contact with buyers
2. the difference-maker
3. the long-term brand ambassadors
4. the Merchant Default Contact
5. the buyer's encrypted email address
6. the odds of succeeding

II. Translate the contact reasons in the following picture.

Contact Buyer

< Back to Manage Orders   Help

Send message to Jeanette

1. Select contact reason

- ○ Confirm order details
  Ask your customer a specific order-related question prior to shipping their order.

- ○ Coordinate large or heavy item shipping
  Contact your customer to arrange delivery of the order or confirm contact details needed to complete delivery.

- ○ Send invoice
  Send the customer an invoice for the order.

- ○ Courtesy refund
  Offer a full, courtesy refund or replacement item.

- ○ Notify of a problem with shipping your order
  Notify your customer there was an unexpected problem with shipping their order.

- ○ Other
  Ask your customer for clarification for a topic not covered by another contact reason.

III. Answer the following questions.

1. What is the function of Amazon Buyer-Seller Messaging Center?

2. Why should a seller strive to build trust with customers?

3. What should a seller do if he wants to change the email address to contact the buyers?

4. How should a seller send attachments to a buyer?

Ⅳ. Complete the flow charts.

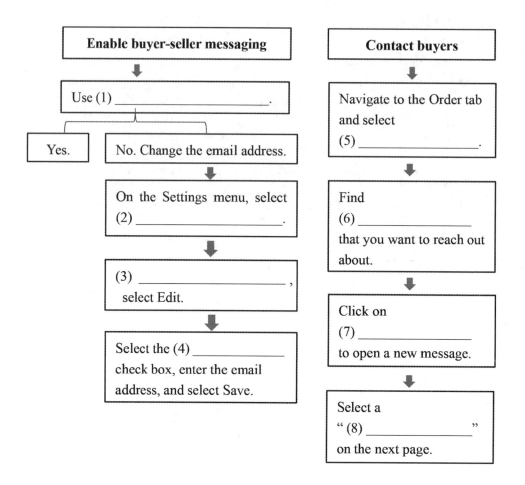

 Notes for 1+X Certificate

Guidelines for Using Amazon Buyer-Seller Messaging Service

If you want to sell on the Amazon marketplace, you need to play by its rules. Engaging in prohibited seller activities and actions can result in the cancellation of listings, suspension from use of tools and reports, and/or the removal of selling privileges.

Amazon prohibits direct emails between buyers and sellers. In fact, sellers do not even receive actual email addresses for buyers, ensuring that they can only communicate through Amazon. Why does Amazon route all emails between buyers and sellers through the messaging system? In an official announcement posted on its forums, Amazon claims that it hopes to achieve the following objectives.

(1) Increase the security of buyer-to-seller communication.

(2) Resolve disputes faster and better by ensuring Amazon employees reviewing the dispute have access to all buyer-seller communications.

(3) Reduce the number of A-Z claims filed by encouraging and verifying pre-claim buyer/seller communication; and eliminate unnecessary contacts during claims investigations.

You will need to keep a few best practices in mind if you send a message using the Buyer-Seller Messaging Service. Failure to observe Amazon Communication Guidelines may result in varying penalties. So, take note that your message may not include the following.

(1) Any links that send the buyer to another website or divert the buyer to a different sales process.

(2) Misleading business names, which inaccurately identify the seller or confuse the buyers.

(3) Improper business names, which contain an email suffix like .com, .net, .biz, and the like.

(4) Marketing and promotional messages.

(5) Promotions for additional products.

(6) Promotions for third-party products.

Task 11 Returns

 Project Description

When customers are not completely satisfied with their purchase, they may return the item for a replacement, exchange, or refund of the original amount paid subject to the product return guidelines set forth by Amazon. Understanding the Amazon returns policy can increase your chances of success as an Amazon seller because you will be able to plan ahead if a return happens.

 Project Requirement

- Be familiar with customer returns policy.

 Learning Goals

- Understand customer returns policy.
- Master the procedures of handling Amazon returns as a seller.
- Master words and expressions related to returns.

Module One　Warm-up

Read the instructions on nonreturnable items on Amazon, and tick the item that is returnable.

Nonreturnable Items

Devices

- Computer laptops, desktops, and Kindles more than 30 days after delivery.

Digital

- Downloadable software products
- Open software
- Online subscriptions after you accessed them.

Cards

- Gift cards (except as required by law)
- Prepaid game cards (World of Warcraft, Xbox 360 Live, Wii Points, etc.).

Hazardous Material

- Items classified as hazardous materials or that use flammable liquids or gases.

Note: Contact the manufacturer directly for service, Warranty, return, and refund information.

Others

- Any product missing the serial number or UPC
- Grocery products
- Items with special shipping restrictions
- Live insects
- Some jewelry orders
- Some health and personal care orders.
- Customized products

Damaged Items

Nonreturnable items that arrived damaged or defective are eligible for a refund or replacement. If the refund or replacement option isn't available in Your Orders, contact us.

1. a desktop no more than 20 days after delivery
2. a mug with buyer's name
3. a computer laptop with the serial number and UPC
4. downloadable software products
5. a dress missing the UPC
6. an handbag within 30 days after delivery
7. live insects
8. a robot vacuum

Module Two Reading

Understanding Amazon Returns Policy for Amazon Sellers

The Amazon Returns Policy (Fig. 11-1) informs that your customers can return your products within 30 days of receiving them. However, Amazon can make case-by-case exceptions in special cases.

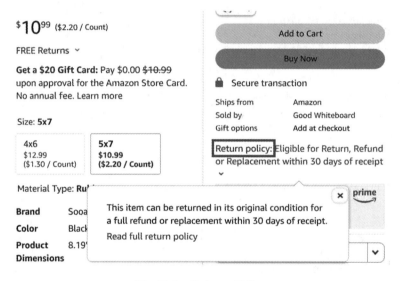

Fig. 11-1 Returns Policy

Let's now look at how to handle returns when you are dealing with Amazon FBA and Amazon FBM (Fig. 11-2).

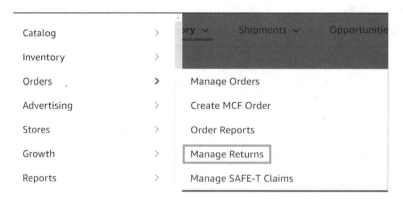

Fig. 11-2 Manage Returns Tab

If you are an FBA seller, you know that Amazon handles returns for you.

What happens when an item is returned? As Amazon handles returns for Amazon FBA sellers, the returned items return to the Amazon warehouse. Here, Amazon evaluates if the items are fulfillable or unfulfillable. There are three scenarios to prepare for in the case of returns.

1) Fulfillable Items

This is when Amazon assesses the returned items and discovers that they are in good condition and can be resold. They will be added to your inventory and sold to the next customer (Fig. 11-3).

Fig. 11-3 Manage FBA Returns

Amazon FBA will also credit your account with part of the referral fee and may also pay the variable closing fees associated with the items.

2) Damaged Items and Amazon Takes Responsibility

If the items are damaged, they will not be added back to your inventory, and Amazon will reimburse you if it takes responsibility for the damage.

If Amazon takes responsibility, it will credit your Amazon selling account with the item's selling price, part of the referral fees, any applicable taxes, and variable closing fees where applicable.

3) Damaged and Amazon Does not Take Responsibility

If the returned items are deemed unsellable, and Amazon does not take responsibility, Amazon credits your selling account with part of the referral fees and the variable closing fees where applicable. You will need to create a removal order if you want the items back in your possession (Fig. 11-4).

However, what happens when a customer does not return the item? Your customer has 45 days to return the items. If they do not return the item, Amazon will recharge them, and you will be reimbursed. Amazon will reimburse you after 45 days. If they do not, you can open a support case (Fig. 11-5).

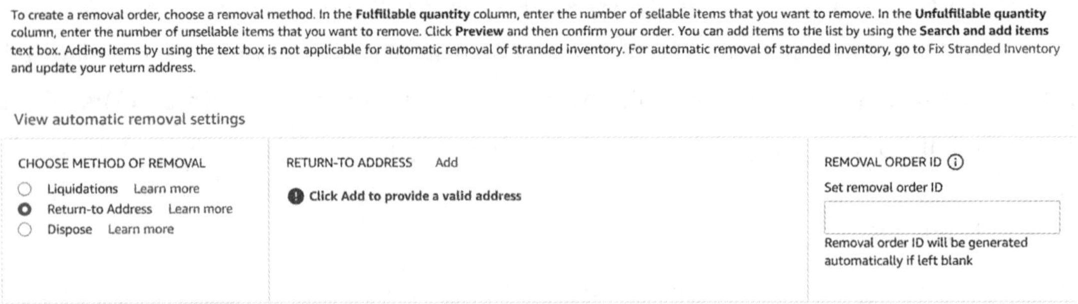

Fig. 11-4 Create a Removal Order

The process for Amazon FBM is different because Amazon does not handle the returns for you like with Amazon FBA. If you get a return request, you will need to match or exceed Amazon's Returns Policy. The 30-day timeline also applies to your customers, and the returns will be directed to the address on your seller account. Once the returned shipment arrives, you have 2 days to reimburse your customer.

11-1 讲解什么是开 case, 如何开 case

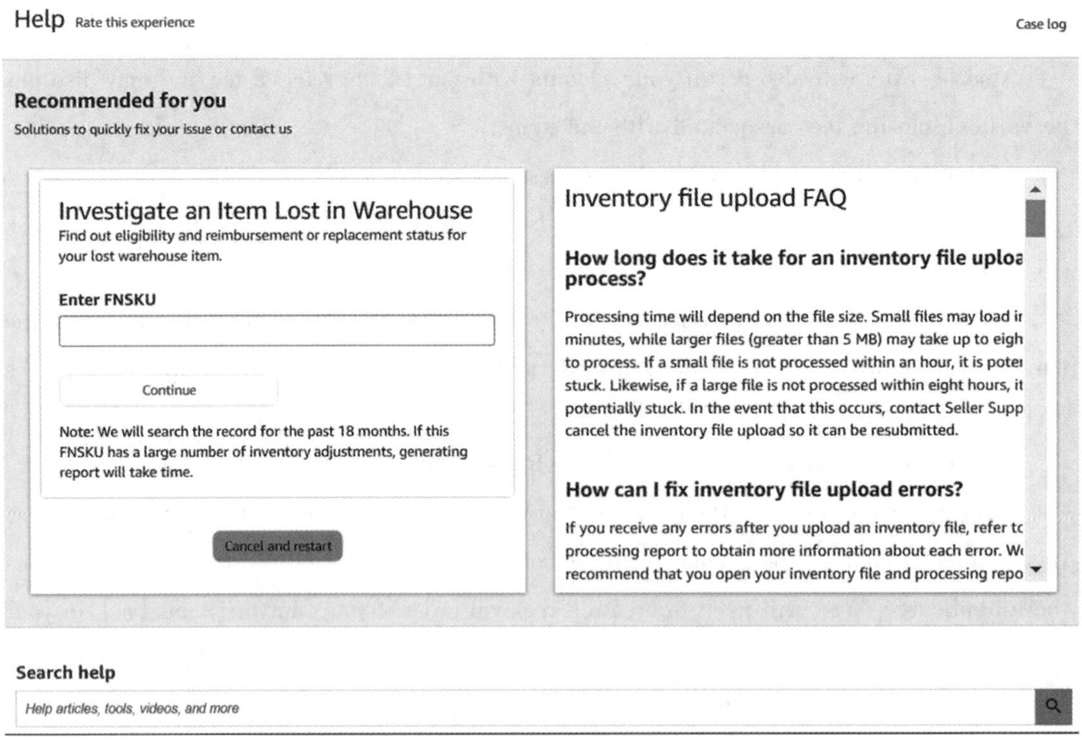

Fig. 11-5 Open a Case

If you have a professional seller account, the refund process will be automated for you. This is because professional sellers are automatically enrolled in the Amazon Prepaid Returns Label Program. This means that Amazon will send your customers a prepaid return shipping label on your behalf once they initiate a return. Amazon will send you a return request for you to review manually if the return request falls outside the accepted return window.

New Words and Expressions

evaluate /ɪˈvæljueɪt/ v. 估计；评价
fulfillable /fʊlˈfɪləbl/ adj. 可配送的
unfulfillable /ˌʌnfʊlˈfɪləbl/ adj. 无法配送的
scenario /səˈnɑːriəʊ/ n. 可能发生的情况
assess /əˈses/ v. 评估
credit /ˈkredɪt/ v. 存入金额
reimburse /ˌriːɪmˈbɜːs/ v. 补偿
applicable /əˈplɪkəbl/ adj. 可应用的；适用的
deem /diːm/ v. 认为；视为
possession /pəˈzeʃn/ n. 拥有；具有
recharge /ˌriːˈtʃɑːdʒ/ v. 再次收费
exceed /ɪkˈsiːd/ v. 超过；超越
automate /ˈɔːtəmeɪt/ v.（使）自动化
initiate /ɪˈnɪʃieɪt, ɪˈnɪʃiət/ v. 开始；发起
manually /ˈmænjuəli/ adv. 手动地
case-by-case exception 个例
associated with 与……有关
fall outside 超出

Terms

closing fees 交易手续费
applicable taxes 适用税款
removal order 移除订单
support case 咨询亚马逊客服

Prepaid Returns Label Program   预付费退货标签计划
return window   退货期限

Exercises

Ⅰ. **Write T for true or F for false in the brackets beside the following statements about the text.**

1. Customers on Amazon can return all the products within 30 days of receiving them.   (   )
2. For Amazon FBA sellers, Amazon assesses whether the returned items are fulfillable or unfulfillable.   (   )
3. Amazon FBA sellers will receive the referral fee and the variable closing fees from Amazon for the fulfillable items.   (   )
4. Amazon seller will get a reimburse for the damaged items.   (   )
5. Amazon will credit the seller's account with the item's selling price and other fees and applicable taxes if it takes responsibility.   (   )
6. Amazon will reimburse an Amazon FBA seller nothing if the returned item is damaged and Amazon does not take responsibility.   (   )
7. Amazon FBA seller can open a support case if a customer does not return an item.   (   )
8. Amazon FBM seller will need to match or exceed Amazon's Returns Policy if he gets a return request.   (   )
9. For Amazon FBM seller, the returns will be sent to the address on the seller account within 30-day timeline.   (   )
10. Amazon FBM seller has to reimburse the customer within 2 days after the arrival of the returns.   (   )

Ⅱ. **Read the text again and fill in the blanks in the following sentences.**

1. Customers can return the products on Amazon within 30 days of receiving them, except _____ in special cases.
2. For Amazon FBA sellers, the returned item will be sent to the _____, where Amazon assesses the items.
3. If the returned items are proven to be in good condition and resold, they will be stored in the _____ and sold to the next customer.

4. Amazon FBA will credit the Amazon seller's account with the returned item's selling price, _____, _____, and _____ where applicable for the damaged items which Amazon takes responsibility for.

5. Amazon FBA seller will need to create _____ if he wants to possess the damaged items for which Amazon does not take responsibility.

6. The customer has to send back the returned items within 45 days, or he will be _____ by Amazon to reimburse the seller.

7. The process of return for Amazon FBM is different from Amazon FBA, for the reason that Amazon does not _____ for you.

8. On behalf of Amazon FBM seller who has a professional seller account, once the customer initiates a return, Amazon will send him _____.

III. Translate the following passage into Chinese.

If the returned items are deemed unsellable, and Amazon does not take responsibility, Amazon credits your selling account with part of the referral fees and the variable closing fees where applicable. You will need to create a removal order if you want the items back in your possession.

Module Three Project Implementation

How to Handle Amazon Returns as a Seller?

When dealing with Amazon returns, it is vital to be aware of the best practices your account may need. Here are some ways to protect your seller account by handling Amazon returns correctly.

1. Save the Return Notification Email You Get from Amazon

Amazon issues a notification (Fig. 11-6) when a buyer requests a return. Make sure you keep evidence of the statements in your email (Fig. 11-7).

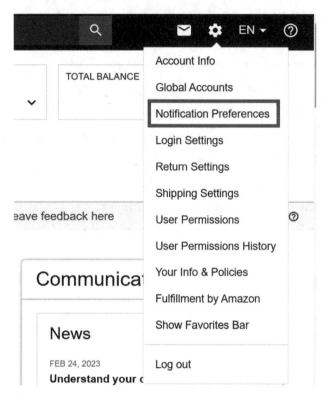

Fig. 11-6 Notification Preferences

Fig. 11-7 Notification Email Setting

2. Ask for Compensation from Amazon

Again, you should check if the items are back to FBA for more details. If Amazon implements a refund without a returns policy, you can at least request some compensation.

"Refund without return" is a policy where Amazon gives a product's buying cost to the buyer directly. Here, buyers get a full refund without them returning the purchased goods.

Online stores are continually reinventing their business models to gain more customers. One way they do this is through the returnless refund policy. In the case of Amazon, they offer this policy as a way to improve customers' shopping experience and minimize costs. But, it is essential to note that Amazon retains the discretion of issuing refunds without returns.

3. Maintain Your Seller Feedback Score

A buyer may leave feedback after requesting a refund (Fig. 11-8). But, regardless of the buyer's feedback, make sure you contact them to show about your customer cares. You can find out about their experience and offer your regrets. And, sometimes, you may get the negative feedback removed.

Fig. 11-8 Feedback Score

4. Do the Return Inspection

Amazon wants to help you protect your selling account. If the returned item was not open and in new condition, they will take it back. You can send these items directly to Amazon for less than $1.

You can request Amazon to allow the product to be returned even if it falls under a refund without a returns policy. Yet, in this case, you may need to bear the return costs.

Ensure you check all items that return to your warehouse. Thus, you can carry out further inspection of the product. You will get to know if it has any defects. If the product is genuine, you can report the buyer by presenting all proofs to Amazon.

11-2 处理退货的三种常见方式

5. Know the Cause for the Return

Checking on the reason for returns is another way to protect yourself as a business owner. It is a good idea to identify what made the buyer return the item. If it is something you can fix, it will save you trouble in the future.

You can check the reasons for the return by running a report under Seller Central. You can access this by going to Reports > Fulfillment > Customer Concessions > FBA customer returns (Fig. 11-9).

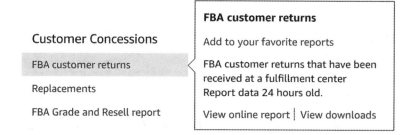

Fig. 11-9　FBA Customer Returns

Customers have various reasons to return an item, such as ordered by mistake or no longer needed items (Fig. 11-10). Also, some of these need customers to pay shipping costs.

Quantity	FC	Disposition	Customer Return Reason	Status
1	EWR7	Sellable	I accidentally ordered the wrong item	Unit returned to inventory

Fig. 11-10　Customer Return Reason

Exercises

I. Find the English expressions in the text for the following phrases.

1. 支付运费 _____
2. 卖家反馈评分 _____

3. 差评_____
4. 退货通知电子邮件_____
5. 下错订单_____
6. 买家优惠_____
7. 退款不退货政策_____
8. 承担退货费用_____
9. 不再需要物品_____
10. 要求退货_____

Ⅱ. Answer the following questions.

1. Why does an Amazon seller have to save the Return Notification Email?
_____

2. How does an Amazon seller maintain his Seller Feedback Score?
_____

3. How can a seller check the reasons for the return on Amazon?
_____

4. List the reasons that customers return an item.
_____

Ⅲ. Complete the sentences first, and then put them in the correct order.

1. Contact buyers to_____, to find out about _____, and to offer _____ for the purpose of maintaining the seller feedback score.

2. Whether the items are returned to Amazon or _____, they will be inspected for any defects.

3. Save the _____ issued by Amazon after a buyer requests a return.

4. Check if a seller can ask for_____ if the returned items are back to FBA, or fall in the refund without return policy.

5. Identifying_____will protect the business owner and may save him trouble in the future, especially it is something he can fix.

The correct order：____ ____ ____ ____ ____

Ⅳ. **Match the return reasons on the left with their Chinese versions on the right.**

1. Ordered wrong item   a. 不想要的商品
2. Found better price   b. 商品运送到时存在残损或瑕疵
3. No reason given   c. 商品存在瑕疵
4. Quality unacceptable   d. 和网站上的描述不一致
5. Not compatible   e. 商品性能或质量未达到我的期望
6. Missed estimated delivery   f. 我意外订购了错误的商品
7. Missing parts   g. 货件中包含其他商品
8. Damaged by carrier   h. 我在其他地方发现了更优惠的价格
9. Defective   i. 服装:商品太小
10. Extra item   j. 我的商品与当前系统不兼容
11. Unwanted item   k. 商品运送时间过长,我不想要了
12. Not as described   l. 没有原因,我只是不想购买了
13. Apparel too small   m. 配送中商品或配件丢失

Notes for 1+X Certificate

How Amazon Classifies FBA Returns

Amazon has a FBA customer returns report that lists the different categories of returns. These are the condition codes you will find in your reports and how Amazon classifies it.

- **Sellable**

Returned items in this category are still in good condition. Amazon will return these items into your active inventory so that you can resell them to other customers. You can decide to verify the items yourself if you are worried about their condition. To do this, fill out a removal order to personally inspect sellable items.

- **Damaged**

Items or products that are labeled damaged will not be re-sold. However, you may receive reimbursement from Amazon if the company is responsible for the damage. For instance, if during transit, the product got damaged because the employee did not seal it properly, then you are eligible for reimbursement because Amazon is accountable in such cases.

However, if the fault is from your end, then you will not receive reimbursement. Therefore, always ensure you pack and seal all your products very well before shipping them to the Amazon warehouse.

· Customer Damaged

Customer damage sounds as if a customer damaged the product after receiving the order- that is far from it. In this context, customer damage is when a buyer returns a product in less than new condition after opening it.

While customer damaged items will not be re-sold as a new product, there is still a chance for Amazon to resell them in some ways. Your best bet is to create a removal order to personally inspect the product, and then decide whether or not it is worth reselling.

Be warned that allowing Amazon to resell customer damaged products will get your account banned. How? If another customer receives the item that looks used, they will return the product with the reason "used as new" which is one of the easiest ways to get your listing and account suspended.

· Carrier Damaged

Carrier damaged products are those products that Amazon's selected carriers (UPS, FedEx, USPS) failed to take care of while in transit. As a result, they got damaged. In some cases, FedEx says delivered but no package has been received by you. For this, you are eligible for reimbursement because the fault is not from your end. You entrusted Amazon to handle your products with utmost care.

This is one of the easiest reimbursements to win back which many sellers do not do.

· Defective

These are FBA returns that are not functioning properly or defective. Whenever a customer receives a defective product, he/she is entitled to a refund. The product will be considered unsellable and kept in your inventory. I have seen cases where customers file for returns, citing "defective products" even when the item is not defective. Most times, they do this to have free return shipping.

To be on the safe side, file a removal order to personally inspect the product. I can assure you that you will find that a lot of "defective" grocery items are in excellent condition.

In such situations, to minimize losses and boost your profits, send the products back to the FBA warehouse for resale.

Remember, overwhelming negative reviews about your brand for selling defective products can hurt your metrics and thus compel Amazon to suspend your seller's account. So, whenever a false allegation comes up, take action to protect your account and your brand.

· Expired

Units that are within 50 days of the expiration date may be set aside as "unsellable" and eventually removed for disposal by Amazon. Units that have been disposed will not be available for return. You may request to have expired units returned to you if they have not been disposed of.

If you sell food or other expiry related products, make sure your expiry dates are updated when you send in a new shipment. There have been many instances of people reselling old and expired food products which are dangerous.

Task 12　Handling Negative Comments

 Project Description

　　As an Amazon seller, you are likely to get plenty of great reviews and feedback. Customers sometimes leave negative reviews and feedback, even when you do everything right. But responding openly and honestly to negative reviews and feedback can help you to maintain your brand image, convince future customers that if they have a problem you can help them fix it, and will help to keep customer satisfaction up.

 Project Requirement

· Handle the negative feedback and review.

 Learning Goals

· Understand the definition and importance of feedback and review.
· Master the procedures of handling the negative comments.
· Master words and expressions related to feedback and review.

Module One　Warm-up

Read the passage and discuss with your partner about following questions.

It is found that approximately one-in-five of online shoppers view product reviews as one of the most important factors influencing their purchasing decisions. Reviews provide social proof, allowing customers to benefit from reading about others' experiences with products. Social proof is particularly important for e-commerce websites, as customers seek additional information about the quality and sensory aspects of products they can not see or touch before placing an order.

1. Do you read product reviews before making an online purchase? Why?
2. Do you leave reviews for the product purchased online? Why?

 ## Module Two　Reading

Seller Feedback and Product Review

Amazon feedback, also known as seller feedback, is your customer's opinion about your business (Fig. 12-1). The Amazon review, on the other hand, is specific to the product, determining its quality and functionality.

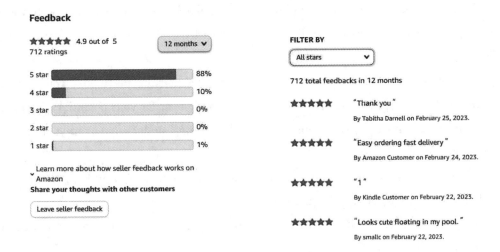

Fig. 12-1 Feedback

· **Seller Feedback**

Amazon feedback utilizes a 1-5 rating system, with five being the highest feedback you can get. This feedback focuses on how you performed as a seller, including packaging, delivery, as well as after-sales customer support.

Your seller feedback affects you in more than one way.

(1) It determines your metrics as a seller. Amazon utilizes various metrics to monitor seller performance and grade their sellers (Fig. 12-2). The higher your feedback, the higher your performance and seller ranking. Low feedback or recurrent negative judgments can lead to your account being restricted.

12-1 什么是 metrics

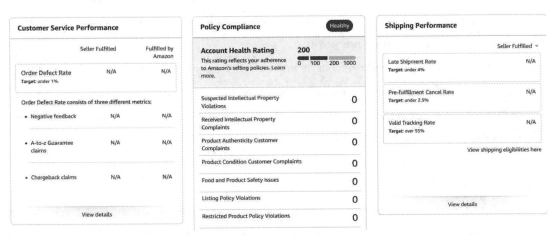

Fig. 12-2 Performance Metrics

(2) It determines your seller ranking. Your feedback tells Amazon how well you are doing compared to your competitors. Based on this metric, it determines your position on the search page.

(3) It influences product ranking and exposure. Obviously, the higher you rank as a seller, the higher your products will rank. This makes it easier for your potential customers to find your product. An easy way to rank higher is by offering stellar support to your clients to get high seller feedback.

(4) It influences the conversion rate and chances of winning the Buy Box. Shoppers are more likely to buy from sellers with a good feedback rating. If your customers are not happy with your services, it is less likely you will win the Buy Box. And your conversion rates will suffer as a result.

(5) It impacts your brand reputation and customer loyalty. At the end of the day, your seller feedback has a huge impact on your brand reputation and customer loyalty. That is why you should always aim for the highest possible score.

· **Product Reviews**

Anyone who has bought an item on Amazon can leave a product review under your listing, which means buyers can leave a review even if they did not buy the product from you (Fig. 12-3). Like the feedback, review varies on a scale from 1 to 5. And besides the star rating, your customers can also leave a comment expressing their opinion and experience with the product. It is a separate metric from the feedback, and it affects you in a different way. While this rating does not affect your performance as a seller, it can have a negative impact on your conversion rates and sales. In fact, shoppers are unlikely to buy a product with a low star rating and poor reviews. Whereas your conversion rate and sales will rise exponentially if the product ratings and reviews are positive.

In summary, Amazon feedback has a huge impact on your seller metrics and ability to sell on Amazon. If your score is too low, the marketplace might apply restrictions on your account or cancel it altogether (Fig. 12-4). Amazon reviews can increase or decrease your conversion rates and chances of gaining more sales.

You should focus on performing well as a qualified seller first. Then make efforts to improve and expand your business.

With this in mind and under the premise of maintaining good performance, you should learn how to win more positive reviews and feedback and how to handle the negative comments.

Unit Four Customer Service

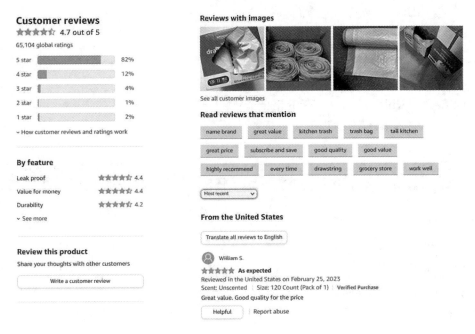

Fig. 12-3 Review

Fig. 12-4 Account Health Rating

New Words and Expressions

functionality /ˌfʌŋkʃəˈnæləti/ n. 功能

utilize /ˈjuːtəlaɪz/ v. 使用

metric /ˈmetrɪk/ n. 度量标准

marketplace /ˈmɑːkɪtpleɪs/ n. 市场竞争

monitor /ˈmɒnɪtə(r)/ v. 监视

grade /ɡreɪd/ v. 分级

recurrent /rɪˈkʌrənt/ adj. 反复出现的

exposure /ɪkˈspəʊʒə(r)/ n. 曝光

stellar /ˈstelə(r)/ *adj.* 优秀的
vary /ˈveəri/ *v.* 变化
restriction /rɪˈstrɪkʃn/ *n.* 限制规定
cancel /ˈkænsl/ *v.* 取消；撤销
qualified /ˈkwɒlɪfaɪd/ *adj.* 有资格的
premise /ˈpremɪs/ *n.* 前提

Terms

rating system   评级系统
seller ranking   卖家排名
search page   搜索页面
Buy Box   黄金购物车
brand reputation   品牌声誉
customer loyalty   客户忠诚度

Exercises

Ⅰ. Write T for true or F for false in the brackets beside the following statements about the text.

1. Seller feedback is your customer's opinion about your performance as a seller, while review is about the quality and functionality of the product.   (   )
2. Five is the highest feedback a seller can get, and one is the lowest.   (   )
3. Seller feedback determines a seller's performance and seller ranking.   (   )
4. Your feedback indirectly determines a seller's position on all search page.   (   )
5. It is one of the common ways to provide support to the clients to get high seller feedback.   (   )
6. If a seller has a good feedback rating, it is less likely for him to win the Buy Box.   (   )
7. Your seller feedback determines your brand reputation and customer loyalty.   (   )
8. Both seller feedback and review use a 1-5 rating system.   (   )
9. Anyone can leave a product review under your listing.   (   )
10. Product review can have a negative impact on your conversion rates and sales.   (   )

II. Read the text again and fill in the blanks in the following sentences.

1. Seller feedback is your customer's opinion about your performance as a seller, including _____ , _____ , as well as _____ .
2. High feedback has a positive impact on your _____ and _____ , while low feedback can lead to your account being restricted.
3. Your feedback determines your seller ranking, which is _____ on the search page.
4. _____ is an easy way for a seller to get a high product ranking.
5. Feedback influences _____ and the chances of winning _____ .
6. Your customers can leave a comment _____ , besides the 1-5 rating.
7. Shoppers are unlikely to buy a product with _____ .
8. You should focus on performing well as a qualified seller first, because if your feedback is too low, your account might _____ .

III. Translate the following passage into Chinese.

The feedback influences product ranking and exposure. Obviously, the higher you rank as a seller, the higher your products will rank. This makes it easier for your potential customers to find your product. An easy way to rank higher is by offering stellar support to your clients to get high seller feedback.

Module Three Project Implementation

How to Remove Negative Feedback on Amazon

Amazon's policies indicate that negative feedback could result in revoking your Amazon seller account privileges. Luckily, there is a clear process you can implement for handling damaging Amazon seller feedback and increasing customer satisfaction.

Here is our 3-step guide to negative Amazon feedback removal.

(1) If feedback violates Amazon guidelines or falls under FBA responsibilities, request removal.

If you find that negative feedback is in violation of Amazon's guidelines or falls under FBA responsibilities (and you are an FBA seller), request its removal by following these instructions:

12-2 哪些反馈属于违反亚马逊规则

① Log into your Amazon seller account;

② Visit this page, and click "Performance" from the left-hand side;

③ Click "Feedback" tab, and go to Feedback Manager page (Fig. 12-5, Fig. 12-6);

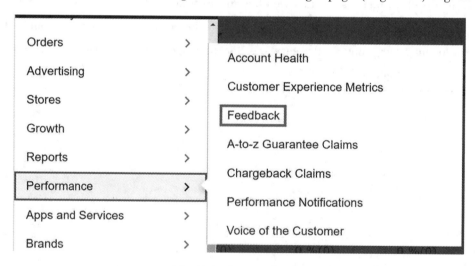

Fig. 12-5 Feedback Tab

④ From the drop-down menu on the right side of feedback, choose "Request removal";

⑤ Click "Yes" after confirming the negative feedback meets one of their removal requirements.

Once you have submitted your request, Amazon will review the feedback and determine whether it should be removed.

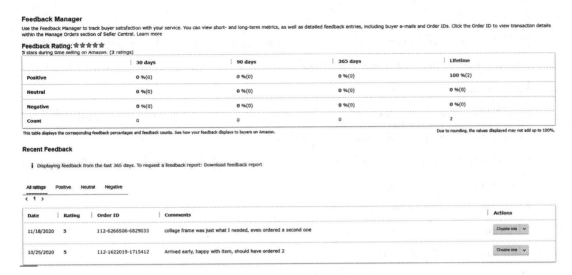

Fig. 12-6 Feedback Manager Page

(2) If feedback is ineligible for removal, reach out to the buyer.

If you have received negative feedback that does not qualify for removal by Amazon, your next step should be to reach out to the buyer.

Amazon gives buyers the power to remove their seller feedback. If you contact the buyer, resolve their problem, and politely ask that they revoke their comments, they may have a change of heart (Fig. 12-7).

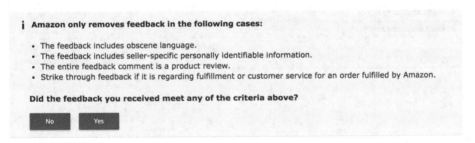

Fig. 12-7 Feedback Removal Requirement

A few Dos and Don'ts of this stage are as followed.

· **Do**

Be timely with your response. Amazon gives customers 60 days after they leave seller feedback to remove their response.

Apologize. Take the time to apologize, understand the buyer's problem, and address it properly.

Adjust your product descriptions. Creating a more accurate product description can help ease the customer's frustrations and improve future customer satisfaction.

· Don't

Don't offer buyers a refund in exchange for negative feedback removal. Instead of sellers giving out refunds, Amazon wants sellers to take the time to understand problems and address them properly.

Don't immediately ask for feedback removal. Your initial message to the buyer should only include your apology and ideas for resolving the issue.

If you'd like to contact an individual buyer about negative feedback, you will need to go to your Feedback Manager page.

To respond, follow these steps:

① In the Recent Feedback table, select Contact Customer under the "Actions" column next to the designated Order ID;

② Type your message (You can also use a message template created by yourself) (Fig. 12-8);

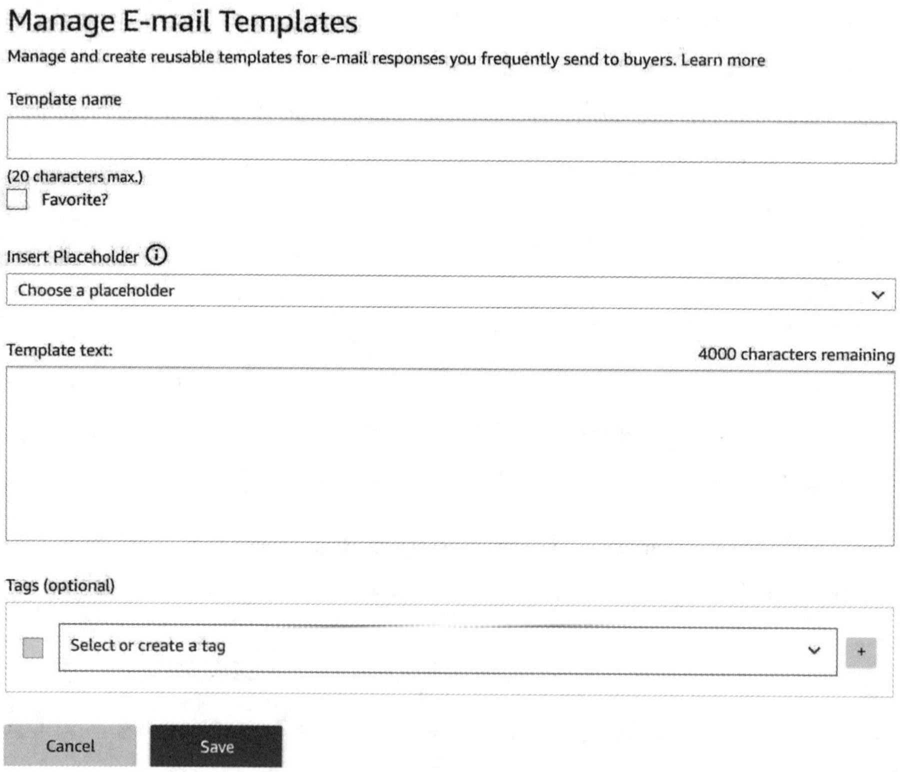

Fig. 12-8 Message Template

③ If you want to include receipts, supporting documents, etc., use the Add Attachment button;

④ Click Send Email to send your message to the buyer.

(3) If the buyer does not remove feedback, leave a response on Amazon's site.

Of course, there is always the chance that you do not hear back from the buyer at all. You message and message, but still no response.

If it is clear that your negative feedback will not be removed by the buyer or Amazon, the best you can do is leave a direct response to the feedback on Amazon's site — that way, another buyer who sees the negative feedback will also see that you made an effort to resolve the issue (Fig. 12-9).

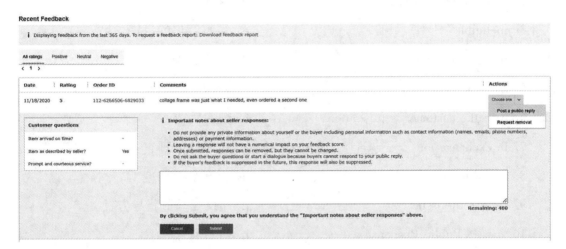

Fig. 12-9　Post a Reply to Feedback

To write an Amazon feedback response (Fig. 12-10), go to your seller Feedback Manager and follow these steps:

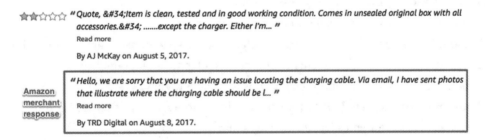

Fig. 12-10　Amazon Merchant Response

① Go to Feed Manager page;

② Find the feedback you want to respond to, and click "Post a public reply" from the drop-down menu;

③ Enter your response.

Exercises

Ⅰ. Match the words or phrases on the left with their Chinese version on the right.

1. feedback removal   a. 不合格的
2. in violation of Amazon's guidelines   b. 撤销评论
3. ineligible   c. 缓解客户的沮丧
4. revoke the comments   d. 作为交换
5. address it properly   e. 解决问题
6. ease the customer's frustrations   f. 删除反馈
7. in exchange for   g. 正确地处理它
8. initial message   h. 发布公开回应
9. resolve the issue   i. 违反亚马逊指导方针
10. post a Public Response   j. 初始消息

Ⅱ. Translate the reasons for appealing the feedback in the following picture.

Select your reason(s) for appealing this feedback
- **Language.** The feedback includes obscene language.
- **Personal Information.** The feedback includes seller-specific personally identifiable information, such as email addresses, full names, telephone numbers, etc.
- **Product Feedback.** The entire feedback is a product review.
- **Fulfillment by Amazon(FBA) Feedback.** The entire feedback is regarding fulfillment or customer service for an order fulfilled by Amazon.
- **Medical Questionnaire.** The feedback comment is regarding a medical questionnaire for buyer to complete before the seller can fulfill their order.
- **Other**

III. Study Comment 1 and Response 1, choose the correct phrases to complete steps of handling the negative comments, and then write a response to Comment 2.

Comment 1

Response 1

Dear [buyer],

Sorry for the inconveniences caused and surely we will try our best to help you solve this problem.

Through investigation, the mistake is entirely our own. It occurred as a result of staff shortage during the busy season and the number of goods was not confirmed carefully. We would like to resend you the new shirt, and you don't have to afford extra shipping cost. More strict inspection will be taken in the next orders.

What's your opinion?

Sincerely apologize for causing you any inconvenience. And thanks for your kindness and tolerance for this problem.

Look forward to hearing from you soon.

Yours sincerely,

[Your brand]

Steps to handle the negative comments.

| A. the differences | B. reasonable solutions | C. customer's need |
| D. the purpose | E. the content | F. customer's dilemma |

Step 1: Study _____ of the negative comments and understand _____ .

Step 2: Determine _____ of the negative comment.

Step 3: Put yourself in the _____ and find out _____ between the two sides.

Step 4: Respect customers and propose _____ .

Kristen

★☆☆☆☆ Snapped heel 1 month after purchase*
Reviewed in the United States on August 10, 2016
Verified Purchase

So disappointed, I wore these heels maybe 3x/wk or less after ordering them early July and then last week, while walking in my office parking garage, the heel snapped on my left one. Not repairable. Looked to see if there was any warranty, nope. Love Nine West but wow, spent this much on a shoe I wore maybe 10x at most. I have the suede blue pair and love them; just hope they don't snap either. *(ps, I'm not overweight nor overly exerting myself on my heels as I walk, I believe this was a defunct pair – SO disappointed there is no warranty or quality control to assist in replacing the shoes)

96 people found this helpful

Helpful | ˅ 5 comments | Report abuse

Comment 2

Now, it is your turn to write a response to Comment 2.

Response 2

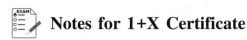 **Notes for 1+X Certificate**

Amazon's Review Policies

Since its start, Amazon has amassed millions of product reviews from shoppers all over the world. Today, 63% of online shoppers start their product searches on Amazon because of its access to this vast and valuable buying information.

That being said, if the marketplace continues to be burdened with fake or inauthentic reviews, this will clearly no longer be the case. Reviews fuel the Amazon selling machine, and if they can no longer be trusted, the proverbial wheels are bound to fall off sooner or later.

Amazon has always had several customer review policies in place, but they have certainly tightened the reins in recent years. Here is what you need to know.

1. Incentives Are No Longer Allowed

Amazon banned incentivized reviews in 2016 and this practice is now one of the most serious offenses. As an Amazon seller, you cannot offer any type of financial reward, discount, free product, or compensation in exchange for a review of your product or a competitor's. This includes using third-party services, websites, and social media groups that sell customer reviews.

2. You Cannot Review Your Own Products

Amazon's customer product reviews policy clearly states that you are prohibited from reviewing your own product or a competitor's, even from your own personal customer account. Your family members and/or employees should also refrain from doing so.

3. Never Ask for Positive Reviews

While you can ask customers to review your products, you cannot specifically ask for a positive review. Many sellers have tried to skirt the rules by slipping this type of request into a product insert, but Amazon quickly caught on and has cracked down.

4. Never Ask Someone to Change or Remove a Review

Some sellers try to get rid of their negative reviews by asking buyers to change or remove them in exchange for compensation. This is strictly prohibited. Buyers may choose to edit or remove their review on their own, but the decision can not be influenced by a seller. Amazon will remove a review if it conflicts with the marketplace's Community Guidelines, so if you see this happen, report it.

 Supplementary Reading

12-3　什么是良好的客户服务

APPENDIX Ⅰ
Vocabulary 词汇表

A	任务编号
a (whole) host of 大量的	3
a good deal 便宜商品	8
abbreviate /əˈbriːvieɪt/ v. 缩写	5
account /əˈkaʊnt/ n. 账户	1
account for (数量或比例上)占	2
acquisition /ˌækwɪˈzɪʃn/ n. 获得；得到	6
additional /əˈdɪʃənl/ adj. 额外的	5
adherence /ədˈhɪərəns/ n. 遵守；遵循	5
adopt /əˈdɒpt/ v. 采用(……方法)；采取(……态度)	2
ampersand /ˈæmpəsænd/ n. 表示 and 的符号	5
applicable /əˈplɪkəbl/ adj. 可应用的；适用的	11
application /ˌæplɪˈkeɪʃn/ n. 应用，运用	6
approval /əˈpruːvəl/ n. 通过，批准	1
article /ˈɑːtɪkl/ n. 冠词	5
assess /əˈses/ v. 评估	11

assist /əˈsɪst/ v. 帮助；协助	6
associated with 与……有关	11
at hand 在手边	1
attribute /əˈtrɪbjuːt/ n. 属性	5
automate /ˈɔːtəmeɪt/ v.（使）自动化	11

B

batch /bætʃ/ n. 一批；一组；一群	2
be on track 稳步前进	6
bestseller /ˌbestˈselə/ n. 畅销品	4
blog /blɒg/ n. 博客	9
boost /buːst/ v. 使增长；使兴旺	3
brand awareness 品牌意识	7
bullet /ˈbʊlɪt/ n. 子弹；弹丸	7

C

campaign /kæmˈpeɪn/ n. 运动（为社会、商业或政治目的而进行的一系列有计划的活动）	7
cancel /ˈkænsl/ v. 取消；撤销	12
capitalize /ˈkæpɪtəlaɪz/ v. 把……首字母大写	5
cargo /ˈkɑːgəʊ/ n.（船或飞机装载的）货物	2
case-by-case exception 个例	11
catch one's eye 引起……的注意	5
category /ˈkætɪgərɪ/ n. 类目	1
centralized /ˈsentrəlaɪzd/ adj. 集中的；中央集权的	2
check out 结账；买单	9
classify /ˈklæsɪfaɪ/ v. 将……分类	4
come in handy 有用处	3

comma /ˈkɒmə/ n. 逗号	5
commentary /ˈkɒməntri/ n. 评论	5
commercial /kəˈmɜːʃl/ adj. 商业的；贸易的	2
comply with 遵守	5
concise /kənˈsaɪs/ adj. 简明的	5
conjunction /kənˈdʒʌŋkʃn/ n. 连词	5
conversion /kənˈvɜːʃn/ n. 转换；转化	4
convert /kənˈvɜːt/ v. 转变；转化	6
convert into 转化为	6
convince /kənˈvɪns/ v. 使相信	6
coupon /ˈkuːpɒn/ n.（购物）优惠券	9
coverage /ˈkʌvərɪdʒ/ n. 覆盖范围（或方式）	2
credible /ˈkredəbl/ adj. 可信的；可靠的	9
credit /ˈkredɪt/ v. 存入金额	11
criterion /kraɪˈtɪəriən/ n. 标准	5
cross-border /ˈkrɒs bɔːdə(r)/ adj. 跨越国境的	2

D

decoration /ˌdekəˈreɪʃn/ n. 装饰品	5
dedicated /ˈdedɪkeɪtɪd/ adj. 献身的；专用的；专心致志的	8
deem /diːm/ v. 认为；视为	11
designate /ˈdezɪgneɪt/ v. 指定；指派；选派；委任	2
destination /ˌdestɪˈneɪʃn/ n. 目的地；终点	2
detail /ˈdiːteɪl/ n. 详情；细节	4
digital /ˈdɪdʒɪtl/ adj. 数字的；数码的	7
dimension /dɪˈmenʃn/ n. 尺寸	2
distribute /dɪˈstrɪbjuːt/ v. 分发；分配；分送	2
documentation /ˌdɒkjumenˈteɪʃən/ n. 证明文件	1

drawback /ˈdrɔːbæk/ n. 缺点；不利条件	3
drive traffic 吸引流量	8

E

e-commerce /ˈiːkɒmərs/ n. 电子商务	6
e-commerce /iːˈkɒmɜːs/ n. 电子商务（同 e-business）	2
eligibility /ˌelɪdʒəˈbɪlɪti/ n. 有资格；具备条件；合适	3
eligible /ˈelɪdʒəbl/ adj. 有资格的；合格的	8
ensure /ɪnˈʃʊə(r)/ v. 确保	5
essential /ɪˈsenʃl/ adj. 本质的；必不可少的；极其重要的	8
evaluate /ɪˈvæljueɪt/ v. 估计；评价	11
exceed /ɪkˈsiːd/ v. 超过；超越	11
exclude /ɪkˈskluːd/ v. 排除（……的可能性）；不包括	8
expand /ɪkˈspænd/ n. 发展（业务）	1
exposure /ɪkˈspəʊʒə(r)/ n. 曝光	12
express /ɪkˈspres/ n. 快件服务；快递服务；快运服务	2
external /ɪkˈstɜːnl/ adj. 外部的；外面的	7

F

fall outside 超出	11
fee /fiː/ n. 费用	1
fill out 填写	1
filter /ˈfɪltə(r)/ v. 筛选；过滤	4
first point-of-call 首要措施	9
follower /ˈfɒləʊə(r)/ n. 跟随者；粉丝	9
forward slash 正斜杠	5
fulfillable /fʊlˈfɪləbl/ adj. 可配送的	11
functionality /ˌfʌŋkʃəˈnæləti/ n. 功能	12

G

grade /greɪd/ v. 分级 — 12

H

hands-off /ˌhændz ˈɒf/ adj. 不介入的；放手的 — 3

have a keen eye for detail 善于观察细节 — 4

have access to (使用的)机会，权利 — 1

high-intent 有强烈意向的 — 8

highlight /ˈhaɪlaɪt/ v. 突出；强调 — 6

I

identify /aɪˈdentɪfaɪ/ v. 确认；认出 — 5

implement /ˈɪmplɪment/ n. 贯彻；执行 — 4

in advance 提前；事先，预先 — 2

incline /ɪnˈklaɪn/ v. (使)倾向于 — 4

initiate /ɪˈnɪʃieɪt, ɪˈnɪʃiət/ v. 开始；发起 — 11

inventory /ˈɪnvəntəri/ n. 库存 — 1

investment /ɪnˈvestmənt/ n. 投资；投资额；投资物 — 7

issue /ˈɪʃuː/ n. 问题 — 3

item /ˈaɪtəm/ n. 商品；项目 — 1

L

layout /ˈleɪaʊt/ n. 布局 — 4

length /leŋθ/ n. 长度 — 5

logistics /ləˈdʒɪstɪks/ n. 物流；组织工作；后勤 — 2

loop /luːp/ v. 使成环；使绕成圈 — 7

loyal /ˈlɔɪəl/ adj. 忠诚的 — 6

loyalty /ˈlɔɪəlti/ n. 忠诚；忠实 — 7

M

majority /məˈdʒɒrəti/ n. 大部分；大多数 — 3

manually /ˈmænjuəli/ adv. 手动地 — 11

marketing strategy 营销策略 — 7

marketplace /ˈmɑːkɪtpleɪs/ n. 市场竞争 — 12

maximum /ˈmæksɪməm/ n. 最大量 — 1

measurement /ˈmeʒəmənt/ n. 度量 — 5

merchant /ˈmɜːtʃənt/ n. 商人；批发商；(尤指)进出口批发商 — 2

metric /ˈmetrɪk/ n. 度量标准 — 12

mode /məʊd/ n. 方式；做法；方法 — 2

monitor /ˈmɒnɪtə(r)/ v. 监视 — 12

myriad /ˈmɪriəd/ n. 大量；无数 — 7

N

navigate /ˈnævɪgeɪt/ v. (网站)导航 — 4

numeral /ˈnjuːmərəl/ n. 数字 — 5

numerous /ˈnjuːmərəs/ adj. 很多的；众多的；许多的 — 8

O

optimization /ˌɒptɪmaɪˈzeɪʃn/ n. 优化 — 7

option /ˈɒpʃn/ n. 可选择的事物；选择 — 3

order /ˈɔːdə(r)/ n. 订单 — 2

overtake /ˌəʊvəˈteɪk/ v. 超过；赶上 — 6

overview /ˈəʊvəvjuː/ n. 概述；概况 — 6

P

pack /pæk/ v. 将……打包；把……装箱 — 3

pain point 痛点 — 6

perception /pəˈsepʃn/ n. 看法；见解 — 4

plagiarize /ˈpleɪdʒəraɪz/ v. 剽窃 — 6

platform /ˈplætfɔːm/ n. 平台 — 2

possession /pəˈzeʃn/ n. 拥有;具有 — 11

postal /ˈpəʊstl/ n. 邮寄的;邮政的;邮递的 — 2

potential /pəˈtenʃl/ adj. 潜在的;可能的 — 9

premise /ˈpremɪs/ n. 前提 — 12

preposition /ˌprepəˈzɪʃn/ n. 介词 — 5

process /ˈprəʊses/ n. 过程 — 1

prominent /ˈprɒmɪnənt/ adj. 重要的;著名的 — 9

promotional /prəˈməʊʃənl/ adj. 广告宣传的;推销的 — 5

property /ˈprɒpəti/ n. 性质;特性 — 6

punctuation /ˌpʌŋktʃuˈeɪʃn/ n. 标点符号 — 5

qualified /ˈkwɒlɪfaɪd/ adj. 有资格的 — 12

R

rate /reɪt/ n. 价格;费用 — 2

reach out 伸出手;联系 — 9

recharge /ˌriːˈtʃɑːdʒ/ v. 再次收费 — 11

recurrent /rɪˈkʌrənt/ adj. 反复出现的 — 12

region /ˈriːdʒən/ n. (通常界限不明的)地区,区域,地方 — 2

register /ˈredʒɪstə/ v. 注册 — 1

reimburse /ˌriːɪmˈbɜːs/ v. 补偿 — 11

rely on 依靠 — 6

remove /rɪˈmuːv/ v. 去除 — 6

represent /ˌreprɪˈzent/ v. 代表 — 4

reputable /ˈrepjətəbl/ adj. 有信誉的;声誉好的 — 9

requirement /rɪˈkwaɪəmənt/ n. 必要条件;必备的条件 — 5

resource /rɪˈsɔːs/ n. 资源;物力;财力 — 3

restricted /rɪˈstrɪktɪd/ *adj.* 受限制的	1
restriction /rɪˈstrɪkʃn/ *n.* 限制规定	12
retailer /ˈriːteɪlə(r)/ *n.* 零售商；零售店	3
return /rɪˈtɜːn/ *n.* 退货	3

S

scan /skæn/ *n.* 扫描	1
scenario /səˈnɑːriəʊ/ *n.* 可能发生的情况	11
seamless /ˈsiːmləs/ *n.* 无缝的	4
search engine 搜索引擎	4
self-service 自助式	8
set up 设置	1
share /ʃeə(r)/ *n.* （在多人参加的活动中所占的）股份	2
sign up 注册	1
signal /ˈsɪgnəl/ *v.* 表明；预示；表达；表示；显示	9
social media 多媒体	7
social platform 社交平台	9
sound /saʊnd/ *adj.* 正确的	6
source /sɔːs/ *v.* 寻找（产品或原料的）货源	3
stand out 脱颖而出	7
stellar /ˈstelə(r)/ *adj.* 优秀的	12
storage /ˈstɔːrɪdʒ/ *n.* 贮存，贮藏（空间）	2
strategy /ˈstrætədʒi/ *n.* 策略；计策；行动计划；策划；规划	7
stuff /stʌf/ *v.* 填满；装满	6
style up 装饰，使……个性化	7
subjective /səbˈdʒektɪv/ *adj.* 主观的	5
submission /səbˈmɪʃn/ *n.* 提交	6
subscriber /səbˈskraɪbə(r)/ *n.* （报刊的）订阅人；订购人	9

subscription /səbˈskrɪpʃən/ n. 订阅，订购　　　　　　　　　　　　　1

supplier /səˈplaɪə(r)/ n. 供应者；供应商；供货方　　　　　　　　3

suppress /səˈpres/ v. 阻止；抑制　　　　　　　　　　　　　　　5

T

take up 占用，花费（时间、空间或精力）　　　　　　　　　　　3

template /ˈtempleɪt/ n. 样板；模板　　　　　　　　　　　　　　6

tempt /tempt/ v. 引诱；诱惑　　　　　　　　　　　　　　　　　8

thorough /ˈθʌrə/ adj. 仔细周到　　　　　　　　　　　　　　　　4

timeliness /ˈtaɪmlɪnɪs/ n. 时间性；及时性　　　　　　　　　　　2

U

ultimate /ˈʌltɪmət/ adj. 最终的；终极的；最好（或坏、伟大、重要等）的　　7

unfulfillable /ˌʌnfʊlˈfɪləbl/ adj. 无法配送的　　　　　　　　　11

upload /ˌʌpˈləʊd/ v. 上传　　　　　　　　　　　　　　　　　　4

utilize /ˈjuːtəlaɪz/ v. 使用　　　　　　　　　　　　　　　　　　12

V

variation /ˌveəriˈeɪʃn/ n. 变体　　　　　　　　　　　　　　　　5

vary /ˈveəri/ v. 变化　　　　　　　　　　　　　　　　　　　　12

vary /ˈveəri/ v. （根据情况）变化，变更，改变　　　　　　　　　3

vast /vɑːst/ adj. 大量的　　　　　　　　　　　　　　　　　　　6

violate /ˈvaɪəleɪt/ v. 违反　　　　　　　　　　　　　　　　　　5

W

warehouse /ˈweəhaʊs/ n. 仓库；货栈；货仓　　　　　　　　　　2

APPENDIX II
Term 术语表

	任务编号
Amazon Advertising 亚马逊广告	7
Amazon Discounts 亚马逊打折活动	8
Amazon Lightning Deals 亚马逊秒杀活动	8
Amazon Prime 亚马逊 Prime 会员	8
Amazon Promotion 亚马逊促销活动	8
Amazon Seller Central 亚马逊卖家平台	1
Amazon SEO 亚马逊搜索引擎优化	7
Amazon's fulfillment service 亚马逊物流服务	1
applicable taxes 适用税款	11
ASCII (American Standard Code for Information Interchange) 美国信息交换标准代码	5
ASIN (Amazon Standard Identification Number) 亚马逊标准商品编码	5
back-end 后端	7
bank account number 银行账号	1
bank account statement 银行对账单	1

bank routing number 银行识别码	1
brand logo 品牌标志	8
brand reputation 品牌声誉	12
bullet points 五点描述	6
business license 营业执照	1
Buy Box 黄金购物车	12
child ASIN 子 ASIN	5
China Post 中国邮政	2
closing fees 交易手续费	11
commercial express 商业快递	2
conversion rate 转化率	4
CPC ads 点击付费广告	8
credit card statement 信用卡对账单	1
customer acquisition 客户体验	6
customer loyalty 客户忠诚度	12
deals site 折扣网站	9
detail page 详情页	5
e-mail marketing 电子邮件营销	7
ePacket e 邮宝	2
Facebook 脸书（社交网站）	9
front-end 前端	7
Fulfilled by Merchant（FBM）亚马逊卖家自配送	3
Fulfillment by Amazon（FBA）亚马逊物流	3
fulfillment fee 执行费	3
Google search ads 谷歌搜索广告	9
government-issued national ID 政府发放的国民身份证	1
Individual selling plan 个人销售计划	1

influencer marketing 网红营销	7
Instagram 照片墙(社交网站)	9
landing page 登录页	9
listing optimization 产品页面优化	7
merchant name 店铺名称	5
offsite marketing strategy 站外营销策略	9
off-store marketing 站外营销	7
organic ranking 自然排名;生态排名	7
organic traffic 自然流量	9
overseas warehouse 海外仓库	2
PPC campaign 点击付费广告营销活动	7
Prepaid Returns Label Program 预付费退货标签计划	11
product description 产品描述	4
product listing 产品刊登;产品页面	6
professional selling plan 专业销售计划	1
rating system 评级系统	12
referral fee 销售佣金	3
removal order 移除订单	11
return window 退货期限	11
search page 搜索页面	12
Seller Central 卖家平台	6
seller ranking 卖家排名	12
Slickdeals 简称 SD,目前美国最大、最具影响力的折扣信息分享交流平台	9
special line 专线	2
sponsored ads 赞助广告	8
Sponsored Brands 品牌推广	8

Sponsored Display 展示型推广	8
Sponsored Products 商品推广	8
storage fee 库存仓储费	3
subscription fee 订阅费	3
support case 咨询亚马逊客服	11
TikTok 抖音（社交网站）	9
YouTube 油管（社交网站）	9

课文参考译文

任务一

模块二

在亚马逊上销售前您必须知道的事情

如果您想扩大公司的销售范围,在亚马逊上销售是一个简单的过程。

亚马逊业务是真实交易,因此您需要考虑和准备很多事情。以下是您开始亚马逊卖家职业生涯所需的文件和信息。在亚马逊上注册卖家账户之前,请确保有这些信息:

(1)信用卡信息;

(2)银行账号;

(3)银行识别码;

(4)营业执照;

(5)电话号码。

亚马逊会要求您提供其他文件,如银行账户对账单、信用卡对账单、政府颁发的国民身份证等其他文件的扫描件。

要成为亚马逊卖家,您必须在亚马逊卖家平台注册并创建亚马逊卖家账户。您需要选择销售计划的类型。目前,亚马逊上有两种销售计划:个人销售计划和专业销售计划。

个人销售计划(个人卖家账户):该账户没有月费,但您一个月最多可以卖出40件商品,可销售20个类目的产品。每卖出一件商品,平台会收取0.99美元。如果您选择个人账户,您可以保持低成本。然而,它也有许多缺点,例如,您将无法在亚马逊上为您的产品做广告。

专业销售计划(专业卖家账户):每月订阅费为39.99美元,每月销售商品数量可超过40件。专业账户持有人可以销售任何类目的产品。但是,有些受限类目只有在平台批准后才能销售。作为一名专业的卖家,您将获得许多销售工具,以帮助您经营业务和管理库存。

首先,创建一个账户并填写所有必要的信息。其次,添加产品页面,并选择是自己发货还是使用亚马逊的仓储配送服务。一旦一切就绪,您就可以开卖了!

模块三

创建亚马逊卖家账户指南

一旦您确定了在亚马逊上销售的计划,您就需要完成亚马逊卖家注册流程。访问 https://sell.amazon.com,注册成为亚马逊卖家。单击注册,创建一个新账户。

1. 选择您的"业务地点"和"业务类型"
2. 您的营业地点是指您的企业所在的国家

您的业务类型是指您的业务实体,可从以下选项中选择:

(1)国有企业;

(2)公有企业;

(3)私营企业;

(4)慈善机构。

3. 完成收集个人信息的五步向导

步骤1:输入企业信息,例如,您的企业名称、公司注册号、企业地址、邮政编码。然后通过短信或电话提供您的电话号码并用PIN码验证。

步骤2:输入卖家信息,例如,您的全名、国籍、出生国、出生日期、居住地址和电话号码,以便验证。

步骤3:输入账单信息。首先,验证银行信息,包括您的银行账户持有人姓名、九位数的银行识别码、银行账号和有效的信用卡号。其次,您需要输入您的信用卡详细信息,包括您的信用卡号、有效日期、持卡人姓名和账单地址。

步骤4:添加您的产品和亚马逊商店的信息,如下所示。
(1)您的亚马逊商店的名称;
(2)您的产品是否具有通用产品代码(UPC);
(3)您是否是所销售产品的制造商和/或品牌所有者;
(4)您在亚马逊上销售的品牌产品是否拥有政府注册商标。

步骤5:身份验证。您需要通过上传身份证(执照或护照)和营业执照的图像来验证您的身份。当完成验证过程中的所有其他步骤后,您会被要求确认之前提供的业务地址。您会收到寄送到该地址的明信片及验证码。您收到后,在"输入代码"栏中输入提供的代码,然后单击"下一步"完成验证过程。一旦验证成功,您就成为一名亚马逊卖家了!

"1+X"等级证书知识点模块

销售政策和卖家行为准则

所有卖家在亚马逊商城发布商品时都必须遵守以下政策。如果违反以下规定并发布了受禁内容,则亚马逊会冻结账户。

卖家在亚马逊商城遵循公平、诚实的行事原则,以确保安全的购买和销售体验。所有卖家都必须遵循以下准则:
(1)始终向亚马逊和买家提供准确的信息;
(2)不得试图损害其他卖家及其商品/评分或者加以滥用;
(3)不得试图影响买家评分、反馈和评论;
(4)不得发送未经请求或不恰当的沟通信息;
(5)只通过买家与卖家消息服务联系买家;
(6)不得试图绕过亚马逊销售流程;
(7)在没有合理业务需求情况下,不得在亚马逊商城经营多个卖家账户。

不公平的行为示例包括:
(1)向亚马逊或买家提供具有误导性或不恰当的信息,例如,为同一商品创建多个详情页面或发布具有冒犯性的商品图片;
(2)操纵销售排名(如接受虚假订单),或在商品名称或描述中宣传销售排名相关信息;
(3)试图在订单确认后提高商品价格;
(4)人为增加网络流量(例如,使用机器人或付费购买点击量)。

卖家不得试图影响或夸大买家的评分、反馈和评论。卖家可以采用中立的态度请求买家提供反馈和评论，但不能：

（1）通过支付费用或提供奖励（如优惠券或免费商品）来请求买家提供或删除反馈或评论；

（2）要求买家只编写正面评论或要求他们删除或更改评论；

（3）仅向获得良好体验的买家征集评论；

（4）评论自己的商品或竞争对手的商品。

违反《行为准则》或任何其他亚马逊政策可能会导致亚马逊对卖家账户采取行动，例如，取消产品刊登、暂停或没收付款以及取消销售特权。

任务二

模块二

跨境电商物流

跨境电子商务物流是指跨境电子商务卖家通过陆运、空运或海运将货物从本国运输到另一个国家或地区。在做跨境电商时，选择正确的物流模式非常重要。一些平台对物流的要求很高，比如亚马逊。这些平台指定物流平台进行配送，并对物流时效性有一定要求。

跨境电商具有数量少、批次多、订单不稳定等特点，因此从事跨境电商的商家大多采用以下四种物流模式：传统快递服务模式、专线模式、国际快递服务模式和海外仓储模式。

1. 传统快递服务模式

传统快递服务模式是邮政服务，它是目前中国最重要的跨境电子商务物流。其特点之一是覆盖面广，几乎世界每一个角落都能投递包裹，覆盖全球220多个国家和地区。例如，中国邮政的电子商务e邮宝是专门为在线商店创建的。它以较低的运费运送小包裹，因为这些包裹以批量方式运送可以降低运输成本。然而，需要满足几个与产品的重量和尺寸以及产品价格有关的要求，例如，它只能发送2公斤（约4.4磅）以下的包裹。

2. 专线模式

专线一般将同一地区众多买家的包裹通过航空线发送到目的地国家或地区，然后通过当地合作公司或物流分公司进行配送。专线投递时间比邮政服务快,价格也比商业快递低。但国内收货范围有限,卖家只能选择物流公司开通的线路。

3. 国际快递服务模式

国际快递服务是时效最快、运输成本最高的服务。它最大的优势是服务和卓越的客户体验,但其成本高,通常卖家不会选择国际快递模式配送。因此,这种模式在跨境电商市场中所占的份额相对较小。卖家主要选择的国际快递服务商有 DHL、TNT、FedEx 和 UPS。

4. 海外仓库模式

海外仓库模式是卖家先将货物提前准备到目的国的物流仓库,客户在卖家电子商务网站或第三方商店下单后,卖家将货物直接从海外仓库配送给客户。这可以提高物流的时效性,为客户带来优质的物流体验。不过,卖家通常只会选择热销商品进行海外备货。

模块三

亚马逊卖家配送设置指南

亚马逊卖家配送(FBM)是一种在亚马逊上销售的方法,卖家在亚马逊上列出自己的产品,但自己(或通过其他第三方)处理存储和订单履行的所有工作。如果您使用 FBM 在亚马逊上创业,请确保您的配送设置与您想要向买家提供的内容相匹配。

要进行配送设置,请转到卖家平台右上角的"设置",然后单击"配送设置"。此时将显示"配送设置"页面。

在常规配送设置中,选中顶部的默认配送地址。如果您从其他位置配送,请按编辑按钮,输入该位置的相关信息,然后按保存。

转到"配送模板"选项卡。有一个模板,除非您将默认模板更改为其他模板,否则该模板将被设置为默认模板。单击创建新配送模板。为模板命名,因为将来可能会根据需要有不同的模板,这样便于将来快速选择。

亚马逊提供了两种计算运费的方法,您可以在费率模型中向买家收取运费。您可以选择"按商品/重量计算运费"或"商品价格分段式"。平台将相应地计算每件物品或每磅(磅)的运费,外加固定费用。商品价格分段式将根据购物者订单金额计算运费。您可以自定义不同的"价格分段",例如,对于 1 美元到 10 美元的订单收取 2 美元的运费,对于 10 美元到 20 美元的订单,收取 4 美元的运费,等等。

您的运费通常基于尺寸和重量,因此选择"每件/重量"选项通常是合理的。

选择配送选项。您可以选择提供哪些配送选项。首先选择以下一个或多个选项:

(1)标准配送;

(2)加急配送;

(3)隔日达;

(4)次日达;

(5)当日达;

(6)国际配送。

选择要配送的地区。要更改区域设置,请单击"编辑"。如果您在美国销售,亚马逊将允许您选择/取消选择阿拉斯加、夏威夷和所有其他非美国本土的地区。

在每个送货选项中设置运费。您可以给每个订单设置单次配送费加上每件商品运费或每磅运费。单击下拉箭头以在按项目和按磅计费之间切换。这里的选项都可以自定义。

现在,您已完成创建配送模板!

"1+X"等级证书知识点模块

了解亚马逊卖家配送

卖家为什么要考虑亚马逊卖家配送?亚马逊卖家配送是您经营亚马逊业务的可行选择吗?与其他物流方式相比,卖家配送提供了许多优于其物流方式的优势。卖家配送的好处如下。

(1)没有额外的亚马逊费用。卖家配送的主要优势是节省转介费和订单履行成本。您也不必担心向亚马逊支付任何存储费用。

(2)控制包装和运输。使用卖家配送时,您可以控制产品的包装和运输方式。买家对您的产品的第一印象是由您的包装造成的,这种印象是持久的。引人注目的包装将使您的店铺真正脱颖而出。您还可以使用不同的送货方式,例如优先送达或隔夜送达,以尽快将您的产品送达买家。

对许多人来说,卖家配送可能是一个不错的选择,但它并非没有缺点。以下是卖家配送的一些主要缺点。

(1)更多的责任。卖家配送意味着您将有更多的责任和义务。您不仅负责采购和获取库存,还负责订单处理和配送。从中国配送意味着总交货时间更长,物流更复杂,对产品质量的直接影响更小。您可能会厌倦回答买家的问题和处理与后续退货和交易相关的问题,而亚马逊对买家满意度的重视会给您带来更多的压力:如果订单有问题,您的卖家账户可能会受到处罚。

(2)额外管理费用。尽管您不必支付亚马逊的运费、仓储费和配送费,但仍需支付自己的配送费和配送费用。如果必须租一个地方来存放库存,您也必须为此付费。此外,如果您的业务发展到某种程度,甚至可能需要雇用员工或第三方公司提供额外帮助。

任务三

模块二

亚马逊物流

当通过亚马逊销售产品时,除了亚马逊卖家配送(FBM)之外,大多数亚马逊卖家还使用另一种方法:亚马逊物流(FBA)。这是一种卖家(或卖家的供应商)将产品直接发送到亚马逊仓库的方法。然后,亚马逊管理所有存储、包装产品并将其直接运送给客户。它还处理客户服务和退货。

对一些卖家来说,亚马逊物流可能是最有利的选择。亚马逊物流计划有许多好处,对于平台上经验不足的卖家来说,这些好处将派上用场。

无须负责订单配送。卖家将负责采购和备货,准备订单,并将其发送给亚马逊进行处理。他们的工作到这里就完成了。因此,他们可以专注于业务的其他领域,更多地去关注公司的发展。

无须处理客户服务问题。亚马逊负责处理客户服务问题。对于许多在线零售商来说,客户服务意味着投入大量的时间、金钱和资源。

拥有 Prime 会员配送资格。如果您非常关注产品页面,您会注意到有 Prime 配送服务的卖家通常控制着"黄金购物车"(一个黄色的按钮)。这是因为亚马逊更喜欢那些能够保证快速交货的卖家,而通过亚马逊 FBA,卖家有资格获得 Prime 交货。

需要注意的是,亚马逊上 80% 以上的销售额直接来自控制这个黄色的按钮的卖家。它极大地促进了销售。

无须处理退货。卖家不必处理客户退货问题,因为亚马逊会替他们处理。处理退货需要花费大量的时间和精力。

虽然 FBA 有一些令人印象深刻的好处,但它也有一些缺点。

额外费用。亚马逊不会免费提供这些服务。卖家每月需支付额外费用。这些费用包括每月订阅费、佣金、仓储费和配送费。费用取决于装运的产品的大小、重量和类型。

退货率增加。许多FBA卖家注意到FBA计划下的退货率比FBM计划的更高。亚马逊有无理由退货政策，虽然这对买家来说是个好消息，但确实会导致更多订单被退回。

长期仓储成本。亚马逊收取仓储费，如果库存长期存放在仓库或订单配送中心，亚马逊将收取额外费用。费用的多少取决于占用的空间以及存储时间。

模块三

如何创建亚马逊FBA发货计划

如果您想在亚马逊上使用亚马逊物流服务来销售产品，那么您需要将产品运送到FBA仓库，以便亚马逊为您完成订单配送。要做到这一点，您必须知道如何在亚马逊上创建发货计划。只有了解具体的亚马逊FBA发货流程，我们才能成功地将产品交给亚马逊。本文将逐步分解"发送到亚马逊"流程。

1. 选择要运送的库存

登录亚马逊卖家中心，单击"库存"选项卡中的"管理所有库存"，进入库存管理界面。卖家可以通过在库存管理页面上搜索SKU、标题和ASIN来查找产品。

选择要转换配送方式的产品，单击编辑菜单旁边的下拉菜单，然后选择"转换为'亚马逊配送'"。

1) 发货地址和目的地市场

选择"发货地"地址和"目标商城"，以便让亚马逊知道货物来自何处以及将被发送到何处。

2) 包装详细信息

亚马逊要求您输入发送到FBA仓库的每个箱子的包装详细信息。有两种包装类型："单件商品"和"原厂包装"。当发送包含一种或多种不同包装数量和条件的产品包裹时，应选择"单件商品"选项。装运具有相同SKU的产品时，应选择"原厂包装"选项。在这种情况下，每批货物包含相同数量的产品。

如果您选择"单件商品"选项，请选择正确的预处理类别（通常为"无须进行预处理"）。

首次发送"原厂包装"时，您需要创建一个新的包装模板。在这里，您可以输入尺寸、重量和每个纸箱的产品数量。

3）产品标签

发往亚马逊物流仓库的每件产品都必须贴上标签，而让亚马逊贴标签是要收费的。如果您选择自己贴标签，请在"商品贴标方"下选择"由卖家提供"，然后选择相应规格的标签纸打印标签。

4）数量

输入每件产品的FBA发货包装信息后，再输入每个SKU发送的箱子数量，然后单击"准备发送"按钮。

2．确认发货

查看您的发货信息，设置发货日期、配送模式和发货承运人。您需要选择配送模式（小包裹递送和汽运零担运输）和承运人（亚马逊合作承运人和非合作承运人）。小包裹递送（SPD）涉及以单个纸箱到达亚马逊的货物，这最适合小批量装运。汽运零担运输（LTL）涉及将多个纸箱包装到托盘上，该方法建议用于较大货物的运输。

您可以选择"亚马逊合作承运人"或"非亚马逊合作承运人"作为您的发货承运商。在这里，您可以看到亚马逊将产品分配给了哪个仓库。

3．打印包装箱标签

打印包装箱标签，包装后贴在外包装盒上。

4．追踪详情

如果您选择使用非亚马逊合作承运人，请填写运单号，将订单标记为已发货。

"1+X"等级证书知识点模块

亚马逊入仓包装要求

亚马逊FBA对如何包装产品有具体要求，以确保他们能够销售产品。以下是一份亚马逊FBA包装要求清单。

（1）所有物品必须单独包装。

（2）每个物品和箱子内部之间必须有两英寸的缓冲。

（3）所有产品必须包装在安全的六面包装箱中。封盖必须完好无损。

（4）如果您使用托盘，每个托盘必须贴上四张标签。标签应放置在每一侧的中心。

（5）托盘上的所有箱子也必须单独贴上标签。

（6）每个箱子必须包含自己的 FBA 装运标签。这些信息可在卖家中心的货件处理进度中找到。

（7）如果使用外包装纸箱，您需要在外包装纸箱上贴上唯一的运输标签。

（8）您可以重复使用箱子，但它们必须是结实的，没有旧的运输标签或标记。

（9）使用一个单独的地址标签，清楚地标明正确的交货和退货信息。亚马逊必须有一个退货地址，以便妥善管理您的库存，以防他们必须将其退回。

（10）选择任意一边尺寸不得超过 25 英寸且重量小于 50 磅的箱子。

（11）使用亚马逊认可的包装材料，如聚乙烯泡沫片材、气泡膜、气垫和纸张。不要使用泡沫松散填充物，如泡沫条、褶皱包装、泡沫聚苯乙烯或碎纸。

每个包装箱必须根据以下标签标准进行标记。

（1）产品必须按照销售类别进行包装。

（2）如果您销售的是多包装商品，则必须清楚地标记为多包装。

（3）超过 10 磅的产品、未通过 3 英尺跌落测试的产品或特别脆弱的产品可能需要额外装箱以固定包装。

（4）当包装在箱子中时，每个箱子必须包含同数量、相同 SKU 的产品。每箱最多可包含 150 件物品。

（5）如果适用，到期日期必须以月日年的格式清楚标记。

任务四

模块二

产 品 刊 登

产品刊登是将产品和服务上传到电子商务网站的过程，包括所有重要的信息。它也可以归属为一项数据输入工作。无论您的电商店铺是在亚马逊、eBay、Magento 或任何其他平台，产品刊登就是在适当的类目下输入公司的产品和服务的工作。消费者根据颜色、尺寸、形状、价格等因素对电子商务网站上列出的产品进行筛选。准确地上传产品能够确保您的产品被正确分类，这样，消费者在搜索产品时，这些产品就会出现在搜索页面。

产品页面上的每一个元素都必须经过仔细思考，以便为消费者提供最佳的购物体验。产品刊登的过程还包括选择能代表产品的最佳图片、突出您的畅销商品和新品，并确保用户可以通过您的网上商店无缝导航至产品页面。

访客使用搜索引擎访问贵网店的第一个地方就是产品页面。一个可靠的产品页面对买家认知、用户体验和销售都有直接影响。想想看,这是您给消费者留下的第一印象。当然,您希望看起来很专业、有条理且受欢迎。您的产品展示方式绝对是电商运营的一个重要部分。

好的产品页面可以提高店铺的转换率。您可能已经实施了不错的营销活动,对产品感兴趣的消费者都被吸引到您的店铺。您必须确保产品页面能很好地发挥其作用——让每个消费者都能在店铺中获得良好的购物体验。消费者查看产品时,如果该产品页面中的产品描述内容切实、图片引人注目、导航操作简单、信息完整翔实,他们肯定会更愿意购买该产品。

超过3.53亿件不同的商品在亚马逊上销售,导致亚马逊市场无休止的竞争。即使您的待售商品品质优良,如果消费者无法在遍布竞争对手的市场发现它,它也无法出售。因此,您最好优化这些产品页面,以便购物者能够轻松地搜索并找到这些产品!

模块三

创建亚马逊产品页面

在亚马逊上创建一个产品页面的过程是相当简单和直观的,知道从哪里开始创建填写什么内容即可。在亚马逊卖家平台注册之后,前往"目录">"添加产品"。

在此页面,输入产品名称、UPC、EAN 或 ISBN 便于搜索。如果亚马逊未查询到与此相关的已建产品页面,就可点击"创建新的产品"开始创建。

要确定的第一件事是您的产品属于哪个类目。您可以通过搜索功能来帮助您缩小类目范围,也可以手动点击产品类目,直接选择合适的子类目。找到类目后点击进入产品创建页面。此页面有多个标签,把相似的页面信息组合在一起,这就是内容创建过程开始的地方。

重要信息

您需要填写带有 UPC、EAN 或 ISBN 的商品编码,以及优化的产品标题、制造商和品牌名称。很多时候,制造商和品牌名称是一致的,但请注意,品牌名称是显示在产品详情页的标题下面。从一开始,这两栏内容的正确拼写是非常重要的,因为它们是创建后较难更新的内容之一。如果您不确定某一栏应当输入什么,亚马逊在旁边提供了小的信息图标,帮您找到正确的方向。

报价

接下来点击"报价"标签。您可在此页面录入您的报价、创建自定义 SKU，注明产品状态并注意如何配送。如果您未创建 SKU，亚马逊将为您创建一个包含字母和数字的长字符串。如果您的品牌还没有一个 SKU 命名系统，我们强烈建议您在创建产品之前先创建一个 SKU 命名系统。

合规信息

您可在此页面提供任何与您的产品相关的信息（如果相关的话），注意您的产品是否与"65 号提案警告"和"安全数据表"中列出的产品相关。

图像

在"图像"页面，最多可以提交 9 张图片。这是一个相当直观的标签，您所要做的就是点击选择文件，导航到您电脑上的图片位置，然后选择上传。大多数类目允许您最多上传 10 张图片。如果您正在为某产品上传图片，而该产品存在父子关系的变体，请寻找标有 SWATCH 标识的图片位置，此处的图片便是产品页面变体展示的预览图。亚马逊接受 JPEG、TIFF 和非动画的 GIF 格式图片。

描述

"描述"页面涵盖了产品页面的"灵魂"；大部分优化产品内容汇集于此页面。产品描述栏允许提交最多 2000 个字符。最初，您只能看到一栏"关键产品特征"，您必须点击"添加更多"才能出现更多栏目，最多有五栏。"关键产品特征"一栏的字符限制因类目不同而有所不同，所以最好将鼠标悬停在信息标志"i"上，查看当前产品类目的字符限制是多少。

关键词

"关键词"页面有很多内容有助于提高产品页面的曝光度，但不会显示在产品页面的任何地方。与"关键产品特征"类似，该栏目内容最多可设置五点，但必须点击"添加更多"才能显示全部。重点是"搜索关键词"一栏，因为您可以在此处添加多达 500 个字符的关键词，这些关键词可能并未在产品页面前台发布。

更多信息

"更多信息"页面是产品的所有规格信息所在。这是一个相对不言自明的标签，但您会看到有很多可能与您的产品无关的内容。亚马逊会根据产品类目概括出可能需要填写的内容，所以不要觉得有压力去填写所有选项。我们建议对所有这些选项进行筛选，只填写相关内容，但填写以下选项是创建亚马逊配送产品的最低要求：

（1）重量；

（2）商品尺寸——长、宽、高；

（3）单位数量；

（4）单位计数类型。

输入上述所有建议的内容后，您就可以点击"保存并完成"您的新产品创建。一旦点击这个按钮，亚马逊将给该产品分配一个亚马逊标准识别码（ASIN）。您马上就能看到新产品页面了。

"1+X"等级证书知识点模块

亚马逊图片要求

要想在亚马逊上取得成功，您必须遵守亚马逊的规则，特别是在产品图片方面。您最不希望看到的是，亚马逊因为您违反图片要求而屏蔽您的产品页面。

亚马逊图片要求详细列表如下。

（1）图片必须准确展示商品，且仅展示待售商品。

（2）商品及其所有特征都必须清晰可见。

（3）主图应该采用纯白色背景（纯白色可与亚马逊搜索页面和商品详情页融为一体——RGB 色值为 255、255、255）。

（4）主图必须是实际商品的专业照片（不得是图形、插图、实物模型或占位符），且不得展示不出售的配件、可能令买家产生困惑的道具、不属于商品一部分的文字，或者标志、水印、内嵌图片。

（5）图片必须与商品名称相符。

（6）图片的最长边不应低于 1600 像素。满足此最小尺寸要求可在网站上实现缩放功能。事实证明，提供缩放功能可以促进销量。

（7）图片最长边不得超过 10000 像素。

（8）亚马逊接受 JPEG（.jpeg）、TIFF（.tiff）或 GIF（.gif）文件格式，但首选 JPEG 格式。

（9）亚马逊不支持.gif 格式的动图。

（10）图片不得包含裸体或有性暗示意味。

（11）鞋靴主图应采用单只鞋靴，成 45 度角朝向左侧。

（12）女装和男装主图应采用模特照。

（13）所有儿童和婴儿服装图片均应采用平放拍摄照（无模特）。

亚马逊产品主图

如果主图不符合上述要求，亚马逊可能会屏蔽您的产品页面，而您的产品将无法被搜索。以下是一些主图限制要求。

（1）产品图片不得包含任何亚马逊的标志或商标、亚马逊的标志或商标的变体、任何容易让人混淆的与亚马逊标志或商标相似的内容。这包括但不限于任何带有 AMAZON、PRIME、ALEXA 或 Amazon Smile 设计的文字或标志。

（2）产品图片不得包含任何亚马逊网站上使用的任何标志、标志的变体、任何容易让人混淆的与标志相似的内容。

（3）不得含裸体或有性暗示的图像。

（4）产品图片不能是模糊的、滤镜效果图像或图片边缘呈现锯齿状。

（5）产品占整个图像的比例不低于85%。

任务五

模块二

产品标题必备条件

标题必备条件适用于亚马逊全球市场上的所有产品。产品标题的四个标准如下。
（1）标题必须符合该产品类目对字符的推荐长度要求（含空格）。
（2）标题不得包含促销用语，如"包邮""100%质量保证"。
（3）标题不得包含装饰性字符，如 ~ ！ * ＄？ _ ~ { } # <> | * ；^ ¬ 等。
（4）标题必须包含产品识别信息，如"登山靴"或"雨伞"。
不遵守这些条件可能会导致产品在亚马逊搜索结果中被屏蔽。
高品质的标题是确保客户在亚马逊获得良好买家体验的一个关键因素。以下是提高标题质量的其他建议，我们非常鼓励卖家遵守以下标题撰写标准。
（1）标题应简洁。我们建议少于80个字符。
（2）标题不要全部使用大写字母。
（3）除介词（in、on、over、with）、连词（and、or、for）或冠词（the、a、an）外，每个单词的第一个字母要大写。
（4）使用数字。使用数字"2"而不是"two"。
（5）不要使用非语言 ASCII 编码，如 Æ、或 ©。
（6）标题只需要包含识别产品所需的最低限度的信息。
（7）不要使用主观评论，如"热门商品"或"畅销品"。

(8)标题可以包括必要的标点符号,如连字符(-)、正斜线(/)、逗号(,)、与号(&)和句点(.)。

(9)标题可以缩写度量单位,如"cm""oz""in"和"kg"。

(10)标题中不要包括店铺名称。

(11)尺寸和颜色变化应包含在子ASIN的标题中,而不是主标题。

标题通常使用变体。一旦选择在子ASIN中加入变体,子ASIN的标题就可能出现在详情页上,因此,在子ASIN的标题中包含尺寸和颜色等变体是很重要的。示例如下。

主标题:

Crocs Beach Clog

子标题:

Crocs Beach Clog, Lime Green, Men's Size 8-9

研究显示,消费者会快速浏览搜索结果,这意味着标题不需要为了吸引他们的目光而包含客户正在搜索的确切短语。长标题也比短标题更难读,所以标题越长,就越有可能失去消费者的注意力。

想一想超市货架上的实物产品,它的标题简短扼要。您只有片刻时间来吸引过往购物者的目光。因此,亚马逊的线上产品标题也不必没完没了。简言之,标题应该反映产品实物包装上的内容。

模块三

如何写出高点击率的亚马逊产品标题

文案是创造广告和营销信息的艺术,能够说服人们采取行动。对于亚马逊产品的标题来说,这种行动很可能是就是一次点击量。

当有人在平台上搜索"AA电池"时,仅在搜索结果的第一页就会显示40多个产品,它们的照片、价格和产品标题都各不相同。

和许多电商产品搜索结果页面一样,亚马逊的搜索结果页面显示的信息相对较少,包括产品照片、价格、Prime标志和产品标题。产品照片让客户对产品有了一些了解。价格是便于产品比较的关键点,而标题往往用来确认产品的类型、规格和品牌。在吸引消费者购买的过程中,标题的作用就是提供信息。

看看下列AA电池产品的标题。

"Energizer AA电池(48个)双A最大碱性电池"

"ACDelco AA 超级碱性电池,可封口包装,100 节"

"Amazon Basics AA1.5 伏特高性能碱性电池——48 节装"

"Rayovac AA 电池,碱性双 A 电池(72 节电池)"

客户通过这些产品标题了解电池的品牌名称、产品类型和其他特征,以及该价格所包含电池的数量。虽然这些信息的确切顺序略有不同,但基本遵照以下模式。

品牌 |类型 |细节 |数量

例如,标题"ACDelco AA 超级碱性电池,可封口包装,100 节"。

品牌:ACDelco

类型:AA 超级碱性电池

细节:可封口包装

数量:100 节

结合价格和照片,这些标题让客户确认他们将购买什么样的产品,从而使他们能够点击产品页面完成购买。

创建亚马逊产品标题时,可以在您的产品所属的亚马逊类目中寻找类似于 AA 电池的标题模式。值得注意的是,并非所有产品的标题都包含相同的信息。例如,电脑的标题信息会比 T 恤的标题信息要详细得多。表 5-1 介绍了一些不同类目的产品标题的推荐体例。

表 5-1　产品标题推荐体例

产品类目	标题格式
炊具、餐具	品牌+系列+尺寸+产品类型
小家电	品牌+型号+型号名称+产品类型、颜色
电动游戏	品牌 + 型号 + 产品类型 + 平台
床上用品	品牌 +款式/图案 + 针数 + 布料 + 尺寸 + 产品类型、颜色
浴巾	品牌 +款式/图案 + 布料 + 产品类型 + 数量、颜色
笔记本电脑/台式电脑	品牌+型号+电脑类型+(处理器速度+MB 内存+硬盘尺寸+光驱)

"1+X"等级证书知识点模块

优化亚马逊产品标题

要想成功营销您的产品,您应该优化产品页面,尤其是亚马逊 SEO 优化(搜索引擎优化)。有一些问题需要考虑:优化已经从亚马逊产品标题开始。产品标题不仅是潜在客户在搜索查询中首先看到的一部分内容,而且标题中关键词对产品在亚马逊上的可查找性起着重要作用。

对于亚马逊搜索算法 A9 来说,产品名称尤其重要。产品标题中的搜索词或关键词对产品的相关性有影响,因此,标题是搜索算法中最重要的关键词来源之一。如果可能的话,标题中的一个重要短语可以包含 2~3 个主要关键词。

此外,产品名称一方面应该吸引客户的注意,另一方面要证明它能够促进销售。所以,想想是什么让您的产品脱颖而出,以及它与您的竞争对手有什么不同。可能是因为一种特定的材料、一种特殊的颜色或一个特殊的功能。写标题时要设身处地为您的潜在客户着想。仅仅由一系列搜索词组成的标题看起来并不吸引人。

我们建议您使用"亚马逊风格指南"作为指导,这样您就不会有产品被隐藏的风险。另外,在创建产品标题时,不要忘记使用移动视图让您的产品标题可以完整显示。

任务六

模块二

亚马逊产品描述

如果您的产品在亚马逊平台与其他产品直接竞争,那就是时候在卖家平台创建您的产品页面了。Wunderman Thompson 公司的一份报告强调,在主要的电子商务市场中,63%的消费者在亚马逊上开始他们的网上购物搜索。

亚马逊平台解决了客户体验的痛点。通过亚马逊庞大而忠诚的客户群,您的品牌从一开始就成为买家旅程的一部分。摩根大通的研究显示,亚马逊有望在 2022 年超越沃尔玛成为美国最大的零售商。然而,您的品牌在亚马逊上的成功依赖于您对亚马逊产品描述的理解和撰写能力。产品描述有三大功能:吸引买家的注意力,让他们相信您的产品是最佳选择,并通过购买和订阅将其转化为客户。

亚马逊的卖家平台提供了丰富的知识,帮助卖家获得成功。也许更重要的是,它准确地分享了亚马逊对产品描述和产品页面的要求。您的产品描述应该有助于客户理解您的产品,尤其是它独特的功能和优势。

以下是亚马逊强调的产品描述应具备的一些关键点。

(1)简洁、诚实、友好地概述产品的用途以及它在其类目中的适用场景。

(2)介绍产品的特点和好处,重点关注其独特的性能。

(3)内容简洁明了,以帮助客户了解该产品。

(4)评述产品的最佳应用。
(5)提交前语法正确。
(6)不应提及竞争对手。
(7)文字不超过规定字符数。
(8)遵守亚马逊的所有标准。
在亚马逊进行产品描述不要这样做。
(1)堆砌关键词。
(2)将您的产品与竞争对手进行比较,或剽窃他们的产品页面。
(3)宣传您的外部网站。
(4)对产品细节长篇大论。
(5)包含公司或其他售卖产品的详细信息。
亚马逊也非常明确地规定了他们想让卖家撰写产品描述的格式。
亚马逊的产品描述模板包括三个部分。
(1)产品标题:长度控制在200个字符以内(最好更少)。
(2)五点描述:这是重要的部分之一,您可以在此处详细描述产品的销售特点。
(3)主要的产品描述部分:产品描述部分告诉买家您的产品如何使其受益。在这里,您可以详细论述产品的主要特征,介绍买家关心的产品的其他特征和好处。字数上限是2000个字符,内容需遵循上述准则。

模块三

如何添加和编写亚马逊五点描述

卖家可以在创建或编辑亚马逊产品页面时加入五点描述,步骤如下。
(1)登录卖家平台,并进入您的产品页面。
(2)进入管理库存页面,点击"编辑"。
(3)打开"描述"选项,并进入"关键产品特征"。
(4)选择"添加更多",在5个空白关键特征栏中提交要点描述。
这只是过程中的最后一步。现在,让我们回顾一下创建有效的亚马逊五点描述需要怎么做。优秀的五点描述不仅要遵循亚马逊的准则,而且要做得更好。记住,您取悦用户的空间非常有限。所以,每一个字都至关重要。以下四点建议帮助您创建优秀的亚马逊五点描述。

1. 搜索引擎优化

您已经听说过亚马逊的 A9 算法。这种智能工具会审查您的产品页面中一些内容,从而使该产品出现在亚马逊搜索页面上。其中一个最重要的原则是关键词。

亚马逊客户通过关键词在平台上搜索具体商品。关键词匹配度越高,他们找到您的产品的机会就越大。

但不要试图在五点描述中堆砌关键词,而要创造性地使用这些词。

(1)选择 10 到 20 个高度相关的关键词用于亚马逊的五点描述。

(2)尽量每句话使用一到两个关键词,并让它们自然融入句子,使客户能够轻松阅读。

(3)避免重复。没有必要在一条五点描述中重复关键词。事实上,当您这样做时,亚马逊可能会标记我们的产品页面。

(4)尽量把关键词放在显要位置。例如,在标题中加入关键词的产品页面要比在描述中加入关键词的产品页面效果更好。

(5)在亚马逊五点描述中充分利用关键词是至关重要的,它会提高您在亚马逊平台的搜索位置。

2. 提供优秀的描述内容

亚马逊的 A9 算法偏向于具有高转化率的产品页面。但要实现销售,需要的不仅仅是 SEO,还需要优秀的描述内容来发挥作用。

取悦消费者是您的首要任务。因此,编写五点描述时,请注意以下原则。

(1)告诉用户您的产品的优势。传递一些技术细节,但也要有创意。让客户知道您如何能帮助他们改善生活。

(2)坚持用事实说话,避免夸大其词。五点描述不应该看起来像营销口号,不要宣称您的产品是最好的,用户会通过体验得知。

(3)同样,任何认证声明都必须有看得见的证据来支持。

许多亚马逊用户不会阅读标题和五点描述以外的内容。这就是为什么从一开始就提供尽可能多的信息很重要。

3. 长度控制在规定字符数以内

对于所有要点的长度,亚马逊建议最多 500 个字符,包括空格。同样重要的是,各条五点描述的长度保持相似,保持漂亮、干净、易读,而且不要留下空白的五点描述。

坚持简短且有针对性的信息可以提高可读性。不仅如此,消费者也会在短短几秒钟内了解到您的产品的亮点。

4. 市场调研

在亚马逊上搜索竞争对手的产品页面,阅读五点描述,关注他们所强调的产品特点。

接下来,进入产品制造商的网站或任何其他零售网站,将五点描述内容与亚马逊以外的内容进行比较。

然后筛选竞争中最常用的五点描述内容。

这种方法将帮助您缩小向客户强调的产品功能范围,也将帮助您组织自己的五点描述内容。

"1+X"等级证书知识点模块

亚马逊五点描述:格式要求

以下是您开始创建五点描述需要遵循的一些一般格式原则。

(1)每条五点描述的字数限制为15个单词,最多500个字符。文字不能超过这个范围,这就是为什么我们强调要保持五点描述简短、没有废话。最好可以对产品所提供的主要特点和好处做一个五行总结。

(2)卖家不得在五点描述中说明产品价格、公司详情或运输信息。这迫使您在创建每一行内容时要有创意。

(3)确保语气不会给人过度推销的感觉。不要提出无法验证的说法,尽量保持脚踏实地、陈述事实。例如,声称您的品牌是市场上最好的,这就是一个非常主观的说法,听起来很空洞,您可以想想有多少其他品牌在说同样的话。

(4)尝试按照相关性来排列五点描述的顺序。把最重要的一点放在最上面。

(5)每条五点描述都要以大写字母开头。一般来说,格式要一致。随意大写和混乱的格式会让购物者感到不舒服。

(6)如果语句复杂,不必严格遵守标点符号规则,其目的是让消费者容易读懂。

(7)如果确实需要在一个句子中分隔短语,请使用分号。最重要的是,在五点描述的末尾不要用标点符号,因为它们计入字符,而且在这种情况下也是不必要的。

(8)与亚马逊标题不同的是,没有必要将五点描述的每个首字母都大写,因为这可能会让人分心。同样也应该避免使用特殊字符的缩略语,让人觉得很不专业。

任务七

模块二

制定亚马逊终极营销策略

营销总是不断变化的，亚马逊深知这一点。这家电子商务巨头拥有多种营销资源，帮助卖家在竞争中高人一筹。今天，我们将教您如何制定亚马逊数字营销战略，让您脱颖而出。

什么是亚马逊营销

亚马逊营销包括众多功能，旨在促进卖家成功提高品牌知名度和客户忠诚。但是，如何创建一个强化这些概念的数字营销策略？

有三个主要渠道

亚马逊 SEO：专注于产品页面优化。SEO（搜索引擎优化）用于提高产品在亚马逊搜索结果页面上的曝光率。其实这都是与关键词设置相关，目标是使用最好的搜索词来提高搜索结果的排名。

您可以在 Amazon 上使用两种类型的关键词。

前端关键词：它们出现在产品标题、五点描述和产品描述上，用户可以看到这些关键词。使用前端关键词可以使您的产品文案内容个性化并且还可以提高销量。

后端关键词：搜索词隐藏在产品页面中，用户不会看到后端关键词，但该产品的曝光率仍会提高。

亚马逊广告：是指依靠基于亚马逊工具创建的点击付费（PPC）广告，这对商业推广非常有用。其中一些最有效的广告类型包括品牌旗舰店和点击付费广告。亚马逊广告可以提高您的品牌和产品的知名度。这种广告投放可能很贵，但它可以帮助您提高曝光率，吸引更多的购物者，增加销售额。

站外营销：指的是利用亚马逊网站之外的工具和渠道来推广商品。站外广告可以为亚马逊搜索结果页面带来流量，提高自然排名。例如，社交媒体营销是站外营销策略之一，它创建了一个品牌社区，然后可以传播关于品牌的信息，提供影响未来购买决策的反馈。此外，卖家还可以采用许多其他站外营销策略，比如，网红营销、电子邮件营销、博客营销等。

结语

您可以选择一些最好的促销工具来设计您自己的亚马逊营销策略。一些专家建议将所有营销活动整合到一个体系中,他们认为跨渠道营销活动更有助于实现业务目标。更重要的是您需要为品牌增长制定规划图,并了解在每个阶段哪些广告活动值得您花钱投资。

模块三

设置亚马逊促销活动教程指南

亚马逊促销是一个强大的工具,可以帮助亚马逊卖家实现广泛目标。通过开展促销活动,您可以促进短期销售,为新产品生成评论。以下是创建有效的亚马逊促销策略的步骤。

步骤1:创建促销

登录您的"卖家中心账户",并将鼠标悬停在页面顶部的"广告"菜单上。从下拉菜单中选择"促销"。

步骤2:选择促销方式

在促销页面上,我们将使用初始的"创建促销"选项卡,该选项中提供三种促销方式:"社交媒体促销代码"、"购买折扣"和"买一赠一"。此处将选择创建"购买折扣"活动。

步骤3:"促销条件"的设置

购买折扣页面需要设置三个模块——"促销条件"、"活动时间"和"附加选项"。我们将从第一个模块"促销条件"开始。在"促销条件"设置中,从"此商品的最低购买数量"下拉菜单中选择客户必须购买的商品数量以获得折扣。如果您只想为单个产品提供优惠券代码,请选择"1"。对于批量折扣,请选择"2"或更多。

点击"需购买的商品"行末尾的"创建新的产品列表"选项来选择参与打折促销的产品。

从下拉菜单中,选择"SKU列表",然后单击"创建产品列表"。现在您可以开始告诉亚马逊哪些产品要打折了。在"创建产品列表"界面上,输入您的商品的"产品列表名称"或"促销追踪编码",填上仅供自己查看的"内部描述",然后输入要打折的产品附带的SKU编号。选择SKU后,单击提交。

提交SKU后,您将返回"创建促销-购买折扣"界面。现在,在"购买的商品"下拉菜单中,选择您刚刚命名的产品。在"买家优惠"行,选择您希望提供的折扣百分比。例如,如果您希望提供40%的折扣,请输入"40"。在下一行,"适用于"中选择"购买的项目"。(注意:如果您想排除某些商品或为购买的多个产品提供分级折扣,请单击"适用于"行下面的"高级选项"。)

步骤4："活动时间"的设置

现在我们开始进入第二个模块"活动时间"的设置，这是相当简单的。您只需选择促销开始和结束的时间。这里需要注意的一点就是，亚马逊需要4小时来处理您的促销代码，因此活动时间必须设置在离当前时间至少4个小时后。如果您想填写"内部描述"，这是可以的，不过它完全是供卖家自己参考。您也无须输入"促销追踪编码"，因为亚马逊已经为您提供了一个。

步骤5："更多选项"的设置

"更多选项"的设置并不难，但很多卖家都会犯下大错，并迅速损失库存和资金。所以请一定要注意！如果您保留了默认选择"无"，则无论是否有优惠券或促销优惠码，买家都可以以折扣价购买您的产品。如果选择"组"选项，您的促销活动将有一个促销优惠代码，但该代码可供多人使用。因此，如果代码发布在网上，您的整个库存可能会很快售罄。

单击"一次性"按钮后，将显示更多选项。在"每位买家只能使用一次优惠码"选项旁打钩。您可以通过单击"建议代码"让系统随机生成一个"促销优惠码"，也可以自己输入代码。请记住，促销优惠码只能是8个字符并且只能是数字和字母。一旦您创建了一个促销优惠码，它就不能用于另一个亚马逊促销活动。将"优惠码类型"保留为默认值"独用型优惠码"。单击"买家自定义信息"的高光蓝色链接，千万不要忘了取消勾选"商品详情页显示文本"。如果您不禁用此默认选项，每个客户都可以在卖家的产品详情页看到促销和优惠券代码的详细信息。在页面底部，单击"预览"，您将有机会在提交促销活动之前对刚刚设置的所有选项细节进行一次审核。

一旦您点击"提交"，请记住系统处理代码需要4个小时才能生效。如果您想查看状态，请从"卖家平台账户"中选择"广告"，然后点击"促销"，最后点击进入"促销管理"界面。在那里，您将看到促销是否正在进行或已经结束。希望这些步骤能让您设置亚马逊促销活动时更加游刃有余。

"1+X"等级证书知识点模块

推广亚马逊产品之前需要准备好的事项

如果您是一个新卖家，希望提高您的亚马逊排名和用户评价，那么下面是您在推广亚马逊产品之前需要做的一些重要事情。

提高产品竞争力

广告是提高产品销量的好方法,其实销售与其他卖家产品稍有不同的产品也是如此。如果您和另一个卖家销售相同的产品,那么您可以加大折扣力度、分发促销优惠券或以销售不同的产品来差异化竞争。

优化亚马逊搜索引擎

确保您的产品页面做好了亚马逊搜索引擎优化(SEO)。这将帮助潜在客户使用一组特定的关键词更容易找到您的产品。

了解亚马逊黄金购物车

卖家应该研究学习亚马逊黄金购物车的规则,并使用易于在网上找到的重新定价应用程序来为自己赢得购物车。购物车出现在产品详情页上,客户可以在其中向购物车添加商品。拥有亚马逊购物车可以让卖家具有竞争力,赢得它的唯一方法是您的产品拥有价格优势和优惠,并拥有良好的亚马逊销售历史。成为一名出色的亚马逊卖家才能有资格获取其中一个可用的购物车。

任务八

模块二

如何在亚马逊站内推广产品

当您开始在亚马逊上销售产品时,有很多方法可以帮助您的产品快速销售并增加销量。亚马逊为营销活动提供了许多站内广告工具。以下是一些可以帮助您了解站内推广亚马逊产品的实用方法。

1. 亚马逊秒杀活动

亚马逊秒杀活动是一种只持续很短时间的促销活动。亚马逊秒杀活动最棒的一点是,只要卖家提供的折扣在七折以下,秒杀商品就能出现在亚马逊网站一个专门的页面上。

2. 亚马逊折扣活动

折扣可以吸引您的客户购买比平时更多的东西。折扣活动是推广亚马逊产品最基本的方式之一,同时这种营销不需要花费您太多的精力。

3. 亚马逊促销活动

亚马逊促销卖家可以以低成本提供产品。亚马逊用户喜欢便宜商品，因此使用亚马逊促销这种方式是吸引他们注意力的绝佳机会。

4. 亚马逊 Prime 会员活动

亚马逊拥有 1 亿多高级会员，他们都喜欢使用亚马逊 VIP 会员的优惠福利，这其中包括免费两天送货服务。在亚马逊上，用户甚至可以筛选产品来排除无法享受亚马逊 VIP 会员福利的商品。

5. 亚马逊广告

亚马逊广告是为产品吸引流量和提升销量的有效途径。亚马逊赞助广告经常出现在搜索结果页面的顶部，因此它也可以成为提升品牌或产品知名度和曝光率的绝佳工具。

亚马逊广告推广有三种类型。

（1）商品推广：是适用于亚马逊上单件商品的点击付费式广告。它们会展示在购物结果页面和商品详情页上。商品推广可以帮助卖家吸引正在积极寻找与其商品相关的高意向买家。

（2）品牌推广：是展示您的品牌商标、自定义标题和精选的商品组合的点击付费式广告。此类广告会展示在购物结果页面上，从而有助于提高销量和商品曝光量。品牌推广有机会让卖家的品牌和系列商品快速成为有意购买类似商品的买家的考虑对象。

（3）展示型推广：是一种全新的自助式广告解决方案，可以在亚马逊网站内外的展位上进行展示，帮助广告客户在买家的整个购物过程中吸引相关受众。

模块三

创建亚马逊商品推广活动指南

商品推广作为亚马逊点击付费（PPC）广告中最常见、最有效的一种广告类型，66%的亚马逊卖家正在使用。亚马逊商品推广活动可以帮助客户在相关的购物结果和产品页面中快速找到产品，从而提高曝光率和销量，因此商品推广活动对卖家来说非常有价值。对于亚马逊初学者，强烈建议从自动投放型商品推广活动开始。卖家可以通过以下简单步骤轻松完成活动设置。

步骤 1：登录您的卖家中心账户

在主页上，单击"广告"选项，然后在"广告"选项菜单中选择"活动管理"。

步骤 2：创建活动

从"活动管理"页面，单击"创建活动"。

步骤 3：从活动类型中选择

单击"创建活动"按钮后，选择"产品推广"。

步骤 4："设置"您的推广活动

选择"产品推广"后，可以设置以下参数。

(1)活动名称：给出一个名称，以便稍后查找。

(2)每日预算：列出您每天的推广预算。

(3)持续时间：如果您想在固定时间后停止活动，可以设置结束日期。您也可以跳过它。

(4)投放方式：选择自动投放。

步骤 5：确定竞价策略和广告位

现在，您可以设置广告活动的竞价策略和广告位。亚马逊提供 3 种竞价策略和 2 种广告位。

竞价策略

(1)动态竞价——只降低：当您的广告不太可能给您的产品带来销售时，亚马逊将第一时间降低您的竞价。

(2)动态竞价——提高和降低：当您的广告更可能转化为销量时，亚马逊将提高您的实时竞价，当不太可能转化为销售额时，降低竞价。

(3)固定竞价：亚马逊将使用您设置好的竞价或者是任何手动调整的竞价。

广告位

(1)搜索页面顶部：卖家可以设置一个百分比，亚马逊可实时增加该百分比，让产品出现在搜索页面顶部。

(2)产品页面位置：卖家可以设置一个百分比，亚马逊可实时增加该百分比，让产品出现在亚马逊产品页面中。

步骤 6：为您的产品创建广告组

在这个环节，您将创建一个广告组，然后选择要推广的产品。为此，请选择要在此广告组中发布广告的产品。您可以搜索并添加，也可以输入要添加的亚马逊产品编码标识(ASIN)。此外，亚马逊还提供批量上传的方式来添加商品。

步骤 7：设置 CPC 竞价

在这个环节我们要开始设置广告的竞价了。亚马逊确实给出了默认的出价建议，而且他们将该出价作为默认值。自动广告投放活动提供 4 种匹配类型。您可以为所有

4个项目设置默认竞价,也可以为每个项目单独设置。我们强烈建议每个项目选项都单独设置竞价。

步骤8:添加否定关键词

最后,卖家可以在广告投放之前设置一些否定关键词。为了避免不必要的花费,亚马逊为卖家提供了通过添加否定关键词来排除不合适的搜索词的选项。

步骤9:启动广告投放

单击"启动活动"选项,您的第一个广告投放就完成了!

"1+X"等级证书知识点模块

在亚马逊上投放广告对您的品牌有何影响?

大量客户在亚马逊上搜索商品。事实上,近80%的亚马逊客户都使用亚马逊来寻找新商品和品牌。

无论客户处于决策旅程中的哪个阶段,广告都可以帮助客户注意到您的品牌。通过在桌面和移动设备上具有高影响力的广告位上展示广告,您可以最大限度地提高在亚马逊上的展示率并触达感兴趣的受众。在亚马逊上推广您的品牌(尤其是使用品牌推广)具有以下优势。

建立品牌曝光度

通过品牌推广,您将有机会让对类似商品感兴趣的客户快速对您的品牌和商品系列产生购买意向。

建立品牌数据

品牌推广使用"品牌新买家"等独特的指标,这样您就可以衡量过去12个月赢得了多少新客户,并进行优化以提高客户生命周期价值。

赢得客户信任

如果您将品牌推广活动链接到品牌旗舰店,就可以让客户在点击后进行更多互动。这样就有机会与潜在客户建立更深入的联系。这种联系还可以让您建立品牌忠诚度,并让您有机会追加销售、构建市场篮和捆绑销售。

任务九

模块二

如何通过站外推广亚马逊产品以扩大业务

在亚马逊之外的平台为您的产品做广告对提高您的销售额至关重要，这也有助于推广您的亚马逊商店。要想成为一名成功的亚马逊卖家，您应该了解以下站外营销策略。

- 与网红合作

网红营销可以为亚马逊产品页面带来宝贵的流量。当行业内的知名可靠人士支持您的产品并分享您的产品链接时，这表明您的产品是值得购买的。您可以很容易地联系到从 YouTube 到 Instagram 的每个平台上的网红来推广您的亚马逊产品。

- 社交平台推广

在社交媒体（如 Facebook、Instagram 或 TikTok）上分享介绍亚马逊产品是一种向您的潜在买家推广的有力营销方式。不过，关注您的粉丝希望看到您发布更有价值的帖子，所以避免发纯广告帖子。相反，您应该以更巧妙、迂回的方式推广您的产品。

- 从博客引流

您应该主动去挖掘那些与您产品相关的博客，并邀请那些博主与您合作推广您的产品。如同和网红合作一样，声誉良好的博主知道如何以最佳方式来推广您的亚马逊产品。

- 社交广告

通过使用社交网站上的广告服务，如 Facebook 广告、谷歌搜索广告和其他付费渠道，来为您的产品带来更多的流量。这与亚马逊点击付费广告（PPC）类似，并且在您使用产品登录页面时也有效。

- 打折网站

像 Slickdeals 这样的折扣信息分享交流平台非常适合推广您的产品。如果您的产品受欢迎，能出现在任何折扣平台首页上，那么您将能逐步获得更多的流量，从而带来更多的销量。当您纠结如何推广亚马逊的产品时，折扣分享类的网站往往是您的第一步选择。

· 提供优惠券

如果您恰好在 YouTube 或社交平台上有大量的粉丝,您就可以很容易地向他们派发优惠券。人们喜欢打折商品,既然大家都希望捡便宜,那么向您已经掌握个人资料的群体提供优惠券自然也是一个不错的商业行为。

模块三

如何利用 Facebook 群组推广亚马逊商品

Facebook 群组是在线社群,包含了几乎所有您能想到的各种兴趣群组,有超过 18 亿 Facebook 用户每月至少在群组中活跃一次。这是一个有趣的平台,您可以直接与群友交流。

更重要的是,如果您是亚马逊的卖家,那么其他人拥有的 Facebook 群组可以成为一个很好的营销工具。一个成功的 Facebook 群组可以帮助亚马逊卖家增加流量,将网站临时访客变成您的忠实客户,在群组内推广产品以提高销量,收集有关产品的反馈。Facebook 有数百万个群组,因此很有可能有一个群组是与您的产品主题相关的。

您只需三步即可加入现有的 Facebook 群组,并可以开始与潜在客户建立联系来提升业务。

步骤 1:登录

进入 Facebook 网站并登录您的账户。

步骤 2:确定目标群组

单击 Facebook 页面顶部的搜索框,输入最能描述您希望加入的群组类型的关键词。例如,如果您的公司出售宠物服装,您可以尝试搜索"宠物爱好者"或任何与宠物主人相关的群组,因为他们最有可能对您的生意感兴趣。单击搜索框下方底部的"查看更多结果"链接。单击左侧边栏搜索筛选部分下的"群组",然后单击结果列表中的各个群以查看有关该组的更多详细信息。

步骤 3:加入群组

单击"加入群组"按钮即可加入群组,这样您就可以在群里推广业务了。如果该群组是"开放群组",您可以在加入后立即发帖。否则,您得等群管理员同意后才行。

您加入了目标群组之后,这里有一些在 Facebook 群组上发布促销内容的提示。

(1)认真阅读您加入的每个群的规则并遵守!违反规则不仅会让您被踢出群,还可能会在您的社群中造成坏名声。

（2）在决定写什么广告文案类型之前，您应该花点时间了解一下这个群组的基本情况和风格。

（3）通过在群里发布帖子来建立在 Facebook 上的知名度是非常重要的。创建与时事相关的帖子是促进业务发展的一个好方法，同时您还得确保在群里积极参与互动。

（4）提供有价值的信息，而不是马上直接带货。您的读者需要的是与他们兴趣相关的信息。更重要的是他们想要有教育意义的信息和有趣的信息。因此，在群里向别人咨询问题、友好互动、解答他人困惑并分享自己有价值的见解就显得非常重要了。

（5）始终记得在您的帖子中添加一点幽默成分。幽默的文案在营销广告中总是占有一席之地。如果您做得好，它可以吸引注意力，也可以吸引观众更多地了解您的业务。

（6）如果您正在群里推广亚马逊产品，请向群友解释说明发布链接或促销的原因，因为没有人是为了讨厌的垃圾链接或广告而加群的。

"1+X"等级证书知识点模块

在 Instagram 上推广亚马逊产品的注意事项

社交媒体是宣传亚马逊产品的强大工具，Instagram 是大多数卖家的首选，因为与其他社交媒体平台相比，它的参与率最高。在 Instagram 上推广亚马逊产品来提高流量和销售额，我们要注意以下几点。

（1）聘请专业摄影师拍摄产品图，因为他们会知道如何巧妙地利用照明、如何选择合适的角度以及如何正确审美。

（2）在您的帖子中使用朗朗上口、诙谐有趣的标题。良好的幽默感可以在很大程度上吸引观众的注意力。

（3）无论您在 Instagram 上发布什么帖子，都要尽可能保持一致，并定期发布。这会让您越来越受欢迎。不定期地发帖会导致您的关注者失去兴趣，所以您应该让粉丝们经常与您发的帖子保持互动。

（4）保持您的账户对公众开放。拥有私人账户只会缩小您的受众范围，不是每个人都愿意发送请求并等待通过的。当您的账号是公开状态时，网友可以更容易地关注、查看和点赞您的帖子。您的帖子甚至可能会显示给之前并不关注您的人，从而使您能够更有效地推广您的品牌信息。

（5）不要忘记在您的 Instagram 帖子中提供亚马逊产品的链接，以便感兴趣的买家轻松访问您的商品页面并购买。

（6）与其他品牌合作。您可以和类似的品牌合作来推广您自己的产品，也可以为其他品牌推广产品作为交换。通过这种方式，您可以有效地接触到更广泛的受众，并提高品牌的知名度。

（7）与 Instagram 上拥有庞大粉丝基础的网红合作。如果卖家想要在产品的流量和销售额方面显著提升，网红营销可能会非常有益。当网红在 Instagram 上发布产品时，他们的粉丝一定会查看产品内容并购买。

任务十

模块二

如何回答亚马逊客户问题

客户服务是业务成功不可或缺的一部分，尤其是在亚马逊。良好的客户体验不仅有助于留住客户，而且会增加您获得积极反馈和评价的机会。

您最不希望的是客户对购物体验留下负面反馈。卖家反馈会影响您的整体账户状况和评级，因此采取措施保持正面的客户反馈很重要。

如果您使用亚马逊物流服务，亚马逊将为您处理大部分客户服务，不过在某些情况下，您可能需要直接与客户互动。

在本文中，我们将介绍您作为亚马逊卖家可能遇到的客户互动，以及将客户转化为品牌忠实粉丝的最佳操作方式。

· 回答产品详情页中的问题

在亚马逊平台，客户可以直接在您的产品详情页上询问有关您的产品的问题。一旦问题得到回答，它们将在您的商品详情页上公开可见，就在客户评论部分的上方。

卖家和其他客户都可以回答这些问题。如果有客户提出问题，之前购买过该产品的客户会收到一封附有客户问题的电子邮件，并可以回答这个问题。您作为卖家同样也会收到一封有关该问题的邮件通知。

亚马逊为卖家或制造商回答的问题贴上标签，这样购物者就知道谁回答了这个问题。

- **买家与卖家消息**

在联系客户时,亚马逊有严格的沟通准则,但如果客户有任何问题,仍然可以联系您。

注意:您不能再对产品评论发表评论。过去,卖家可以通过公开评论来回应负面评论,以补救这种情况。现在,解决和防止负面反馈的最佳方法是回答客户问题。

如果您收到客户的信息,它将显示在您的卖家中心账户中。

您必须在 24 小时内回复这些消息,否则会影响您的账户健康评级。

偶尔,您可能会在这里收到一些垃圾邮件,但您仍然需要对它们采取行动。如果是垃圾邮件,或者您觉得不需要回复邮件,您可以将其标记为"不需要回复"。

- **最佳操作方式**

与客户沟通时的最佳做法包括:尽快回答商品详情页的问题,提供信息,个性化地进行回答,在 24 小时内回复客户信息,为客户提供最佳解决方案,不责备客户等。

良好的客户体验意味着为您的亚马逊业务提供更积极的反馈和评价。

模块三

如何通过买家与卖家消息系统联系买家

买家与卖家消息服务是亚马逊最好的卖家资源之一,因为它允许您与买家保持联系。买卖双方的沟通使您能够接收反馈、提供退换货服务,并从客户那里获得有价值的见解。记住,清晰的沟通渠道也有助于与客户建立信任。信任是将一次性客户转变为长期品牌大使的关键!

- **启用买家与卖家消息服务**

买家可以向您的商家默认联系方式(电子邮箱)发送有关您产品的信息。如果您想改变邮箱地址,您需要完成以下几步。

(1)在"设置"菜单上,选择"通知首选项"。

(2)在"消息"部分,选择"编辑"。

(3)选中"买家消息"复选框,然后输入您希望亚马逊买家发送有关您的产品信息的电子邮件地址。

(4)选择"保存"。

- **联系买家**

对于美国的卖家,联系买家需要以下步骤。

（1）导航到"订单"选项,然后选择"管理订单"。
（2）找到您想要联系的订单。
（3）单击买家名称打开新信息。
（4）在卖家平台的下一页选择"联系原因",或从"收件人"字段复制买家的加密电子邮件地址,并在个人电子邮件平台中使用。

无论您如何联系买家,您都无法看到他们的真实电子邮件地址。电子邮件仍将通过亚马逊的消息系统出现在买家的收件箱中,并在发件人一栏中显示您的企业名称。

您还可以向买家发送 10 MB 以下的附件。单击卖家中心页面中的回形针图标以向邮件添加附件,如果使用电子邮件,请遵循电子邮件平台中的标准附件流程。

现在,您知道如何在亚马逊上联系买家,就可以改善客户沟通,提升您作为亚马逊卖家的成功概率。

"1+X"等级证书知识点模块

亚马逊买家与卖家消息系统使用指南

如果您想在亚马逊市场上销售,您需要遵守它的规则。从事平台禁止的卖家活动和行为可能会导致取消产品详情页,暂停使用工具和报告,或/和取消销售特权。

亚马逊禁止买卖双方直接发送电子邮件。事实上,卖家甚至无法收到买家真实的电子邮件地址,从而双方只能通过亚马逊进行沟通。为什么亚马逊会通过消息系统在买家和卖家之间发送所有电子邮件? 在其论坛上发布的官方公告中,亚马逊称希望实现以下目标。

（1）提高买卖双方沟通的安全性。
（2）确保审查交易争议的亚马逊员工能够查看所有买卖双方的通信,更快更好地解决纠纷。
（3）通过鼓励和核实索赔前买方/卖方的沟通,减少索赔的数量;在索赔调查过程中消除不必要的联系。

如果您使用买卖消息系统发送信息,您需要记住一些最佳做法。不遵守亚马逊通信指南可能会导致不同的处罚。因此,请注意您的信息不包括以下内容。

（1）将买家发送到其他网站或将买家转移到其他销售流程的任何链接。
（2）误导性的企业名称,不能准确地识别卖家或混淆买家。
（3）不恰当的企业名称,包含 .com,.net,.biz 等电子邮件后缀。

(4)营销和促销信息。
(5)额外产品促销。
(6)第三方产品促销。

任务十一

模块二

亚马逊卖家必须了解的亚马逊退货政策

亚马逊退货政策通知您的客户可以在收到产品后的30天内退货。然而,亚马逊可以对个案进行特殊处理。

现在,让我们来看看如何处理亚马逊FBA和亚马逊FBM退货。

如果您是FBA卖家,亚马逊为您处理退货。

客户退货时会发生什么?因为亚马逊为亚马逊FBA卖家处理退货,所以退货的物品会返回亚马逊仓库。在这里,亚马逊评估这些物品是否满足再次配送的要求。有以下三种退货情况。

1)可配送物品

亚马逊评估退货物品并鉴定为状况良好的物品、可以转售时,退货物品将被添加到您的库存中,并出售给下一个客户。

亚马逊FBA还将向您的账户支付部分销售佣金,并可能根据商品的不同支付不同的交易手续费。

2)物品已损坏且亚马逊承担责任

如果物品损坏,将不会被重新添加到您的库存中,如果亚马逊对此损坏负责,它将赔偿您。

如果亚马逊承担责任,它会将商品的售价、部分转介费、任何适用的税费和可变结算费(如适用)存入您的亚马逊销售账户。

3)物品已损坏且亚马逊不承担责任

如果退回的商品被视为不可销售,且亚马逊不承担任何责任,亚马逊将部分转介费和可变结算费存入您的销售账户(如适用)。如果您希望物品归您所有,您需要创建一个移除订单。

但是,当客户不退货时会发生什么?您的客户有45天的时间退货。如果他们不退货,亚马逊会再次向客户收取相关费用以补偿卖家,您会得到补偿。亚马逊将在45天后向您补偿。如果没有,您可以咨询亚马逊客服。

亚马逊FBM的退货流程与FBA不同,因为亚马逊不会像FBA那样为您处理退货。如果您收到退货请求,您将需要遵循亚马逊的退货政策。30天的时间期限也适用于您的客户,退货将直接发送到您卖家账户上的地址。您需要在收到退货货物后的2天内向客户退款。

如果您有一个专业的卖家账户,退款流程将自动为您完成。这是因为专业卖家会自动注册亚马逊预付退货标签计划。这意味着,一旦您的客户发起退货,亚马逊将代表您向他们发送预付退货运费标签。如果退货请求超出可接受的退货期限,亚马逊将向您发送退货请求,供您手动审核。

模块三

卖家如何处理亚马逊退货?

在处理亚马逊退货时,至关重要的是去了解您的账户可能需要的最佳做法。以下是通过正确处理亚马逊退货来保护卖家账户的一些方法。

1. 保存从亚马逊收到的退货通知电子邮件

当买家要求退货时,亚马逊会发出通知。请您在电子邮件中保留通知的证据。

2. 向亚马逊索要赔偿

同样,您应该检查项目是否返回FBA以了解更多详细信息。如果亚马逊在没有退货政策的情况下实施退款,您至少可以要求一些补偿。

"退款不退货"是亚马逊将产品的购买成本直接交给买家的政策。在这里,买家可以获得全额退款,而无须退还购买的商品。

在线商店正在不断重塑其商业模式,以获得更多的客户。退款不退货政策是其中一种方式。就亚马逊而言,他们提供这一政策是为了改善客户的购物体验并降低成本。但是,必须注意的是,亚马逊保留在没有退货的情况下退款的自由裁量权。

3. 保持卖家反馈分数

买家可以在要求退款后留下反馈。但是,无论买家的反馈如何,请确保您与他们联系,以表明您对客户的关心。您可以了解他们的经历,并提出您的遗憾。有时,卖家会删除差评。

4．进行退货检查

亚马逊希望帮助您保护您的销售账户。如果返回的商品未打开且处于全新状态，他们将收回该商品。只要不到1美元，您可以将这些物品直接发送到亚马逊。

您可以要求亚马逊允许产品退货，即使该产品属于无退货退款政策。然而，在这种情况下，您可能需要承担退货成本。

确保您检查所有返回仓库的物品。因此，您可以对产品进行进一步检查。您会知道它是否有缺陷。如果产品无瑕疵，您可以通过向亚马逊提交所有证明来举报买家。

5．了解退货原因

检查退货原因是作为企业主保护自己的另一种方式，确定买家退货的原因是个好主意。如果它是您可以补救的，它会为您省去后面的麻烦。

您可以通过在卖家中心下运行报告来检查退货原因。您还可以通过转到"报告">"履行">"客户优惠">"FBA买家退货"来访问此信息。

客户有各种理由退货，例如，错误订购或不再需要该物品。此外，其中一些需要客户支付运费。

"1+X"等级证书知识点模块

亚马逊如何对FBA退货进行分类

亚马逊有一份FBA客户退货报告，列出了不同类别的退货。以下是您在报告中可看到的产品状况，以及亚马逊如何对其进行分类。

- **可售商品**

此类别中的退回物品仍处于良好状态。亚马逊会将这些商品退回到您的在售库存中，以便您将其转售给其他客户。如果您担心这些物品的状况，您可以亲自检验。那样的话，您需要填写移除订单来检查可售商品。

- **已损坏的商品**

标有已损坏标签的物品或产品将不会再出售。但是，如果是亚马逊公司导致的损坏，您可能会从亚马逊获得赔偿。

例如，如果在运输过程中，产品因员工未妥善密封而损坏，那么您有资格获得赔偿，因为亚马逊在这种情况下负有责任。

然而，如果是您的过错，那么您就不会得到赔偿。因此，在将所有产品运送到亚马逊仓库之前，请务必确保包装完好。

- **客户损坏的商品**

客户损坏听起来就像是客户在收到订单后损坏了产品——其实远非如此。在这种情况下,客户损坏是指买方在打开产品后,以非新品状态退回产品。

虽然客户损坏的商品不会作为新产品重新销售,但亚马逊仍有机会以某种方式转售。您的最佳选择是创建一个移除订单,亲自检查产品,然后决定是否值得转售。

请注意,允许亚马逊转售客户损坏产品将导致您的账户被禁用。怎样会这样呢?如果另一位客户收到了看起来用过的商品,他们会将商品退回,并注明理由"二手商品作为新商品售卖",这是冻结您的产品详情页和账户最简单的方法之一。

- **承运商损坏的商品**

承运商损坏商品是指亚马逊选定的承运商(UPS、FedEx、USPS)在运输过程中未能妥善保管产品导致其损坏。在某些情况下,联邦快递表示已送达,但您尚未收到退货包裹,对于这种情况,您可以申请补偿,因为这不是您的责任。您可以委托亚马逊极其谨慎地处理您的产品,这是许多卖家所忽略的最容易获得的补偿之一。

- **有缺陷的商品**

这些是功能不正常或有缺陷的 FBA 退货。如果客户收到有缺陷的产品时,他有权获得退款。该产品将被视为不可销售,并保留在您的库存中。我见过这样的情况:即使产品没有缺陷,客户仍以"有缺陷的产品"为由申请退货。大多数时候,他们这样做是为了获得免费的退货运输。

为了安全起见,请提交移除订单指令,亲自检查产品。我可以向您保证,您会发现很多"有缺陷"的商品都完好无损。在这种情况下,为了减少损失并提高利润,可将产品送回 FBA 仓库进行转售。

记住,关于您的品牌出售瑕疵产品的负面评价会影响您的指标,迫使亚马逊锁住您的卖家账户。因此,无论何时出现虚假指控,都要采取行动保护您的账户和品牌。

- **期满**

距离有效期 50 日内的产品可能被列为"不可售商品",并最终被亚马逊移除处理。已处理的商品将无法退回。如果过期的商品尚未处理,您可以要求亚马逊将其退还给您。

如果您销售食品或其他有保质期的商品,请确保在发货时检查保质期。有很多人倒卖危险的过期食品。

任务十二

模块二

卖家反馈和产品评论

亚马逊反馈,也称为卖家反馈(即卖家收到的反馈),是您的客户对您的业务的看法。而亚马逊的评论是针对产品的,它决定了产品的质量和功能。

- **卖家反馈**

亚马逊的反馈采用1—5的评分系统,其中5分是您能得到的最高反馈。此反馈主要关注您作为卖家的表现,包括包装、交付以及售后客户支持。

卖家反馈对您的影响是多方面的。

(1)它决定您的卖家绩效指标。亚马逊利用各种指标来监控卖家的表现并为卖家打分。反馈越高,您的业绩和卖家排名就越高。低反馈或反复的负面评论可能会导致您的账户受到限制。

(2)它决定您的卖家排名。您得到的反馈可以告诉亚马逊,与竞争对手相比,您的表现如何。这个指标决定了您的店铺在搜索页面的位置。

(3)影响产品排名和曝光。显然,您的店铺排名越高,您的产品排名就越高。这使您的潜在客户更容易找到您的产品。排名靠前的一个简单方法是向客户提供一流的服务,以获得高评分的卖家反馈。

(4)它会影响转化率和赢得黄金购物车的机会。购物者更有可能从具有良好反馈评级的卖家那里购买。如果您的客户对您的服务不满意,您赢得黄金购物车的可能性就会降低。因此,您的转换率将受到影响。

(5)它会影响您的品牌声誉和买家忠诚度。最后,您的卖家反馈会对您的品牌声誉和买家忠诚度产生巨大影响。这就是为什么您应该总是以尽可能高的分数为目标。

- **产品评论**

任何一个在亚马逊平台购买过商品的买家都可以在您的产品详情页下留下产品评论。与反馈一样,也就是说即使买家没有从您或亚马逊购买产品,他们也可以留下评论。评论的等级从1—5级不等。除了星级,您的买家还可以留下评论,表达他们对产品的看法和体验。它是一个独立于反馈的指标,它以不同的方式影响着您。虽然这个评级不会影响您的卖家绩效,但它会对您的转化率和销售额产生负面影响。事实上,购物者不太可能购买低星级和差评多的产品。而如果产品评级和评论是正面的,您的转化率和销售额将呈指数增长。

总的来说,卖家反馈和产品评论对您的卖家指标和在亚马逊上销售的能力有巨大影响。如果您的分数太低,亚马逊商城可能会对您的账户施加限制,甚至取消您的账户。

亚马逊评论可以提高或降低您的转化率和获得更多销售额的机会。

您应该首先关注一名合格卖家的优良表现,然后再努力改进和扩大业务。

考虑到这一点,在保持良好表现的前提下,您应该学会如何赢得更多的正面评价和反馈,以及如何处理负面评价。

模块三

如何删除亚马逊上的负面反馈

亚马逊的政策表明,负面反馈可能会导致平台取消您的亚马逊卖家账户权限。幸运的是,有一个清晰的流程可以用来处理破坏性的亚马逊卖家反馈,并提高买家满意度。

以下是我们消除亚马逊负面反馈的三步指南。

(1) 如果反馈违反亚马逊指南或属于FBA的责任,可以请求删除。

如果您发现负面反馈违反了亚马逊的指导原则或属于FBA的责任范围(并且您是FBA卖家),请按照以下说明请求删除:

① 登录您的亚马逊卖家账户;
② 访问此页面,然后单击左侧的"绩效";
③ 单击"反馈"选项卡,然后转到"反馈管理器"页面;
④ 从反馈右侧的下拉菜单中,选择"请求删除";
⑤ 确认负面反馈满足其删除要求后,单击"是"。

一旦您提交了请求,亚马逊将审查反馈并确定是否应删除。

(2) 如果反馈不适合删除,请联系买家。

如果您收到了不符合亚马逊删除条件的负面反馈,您的下一步应该是联系买家。

亚马逊赋予买家删除卖家反馈的权利。如果您联系买家,解决他们的问题,并礼貌地要求他们撤销评论,他们可能会改变主意。

本阶段的一些注意事项,具体如下。

· 需要做的事情

及时回复。亚马逊赋予买家60天内删除卖家反馈的权利。

道歉。花时间道歉,理解买家的问题,并妥善解决。

调整您的产品描述。创建更准确的产品描述有助于缓解客户的沮丧情绪,提高未来的客户满意度。

· 不要做的事情

给买家提供退款来消除负面反馈。亚马逊不希望卖家退款,而是希望卖家花时间了解问题并妥善解决。

立即要求删除反馈。您给买家的最初信息应该只包括您的道歉和解决问题的想法。

如果您想联系买家个人,了解负面反馈,您需要转到"反馈管理"页面。

请遵循以下步骤:

① 在近期反馈表中,选择指定订单编号旁边的"操作"列下的"联系买家";

② 输入您的信息(您也可以使用自己创建的消息模板);

③ 如果要包含收据、证明文件等,请使用"添加附件"按钮;

④ 单击"发送邮件"将您的信息发送给买家。

(3)如果买家没有删除反馈,请在亚马逊网站上留下回复。

当然,您有可能根本没有收到买家的回复。您发了一条又一条消息,但仍然没有回应。

如果您的负面反馈很明显不会被买家或亚马逊删除,那么您所能做的最好选择就是在亚马逊网站上留下对反馈的直接回应——这样,看到负面反馈的其他买家也会看到您已经尽力解决了问题。

要撰写亚马逊反馈回复,请访问您的"卖家反馈管理"并按照以下步骤操作:

① 向下滚动并选择"绩效"标题下的"反馈";

② 找到您想要回应的反馈,然后在下拉菜单中单击"发布公开回应";

③ 输入您的回答。

"1+X"等级证书知识点模块

亚马逊的评论政策

自成立以来,亚马逊已经从世界各地的购物者那里收集了大量产品评论。如今,

63%的在线购物者开始在亚马逊上搜索产品,因为亚马逊可以获取大量宝贵的购买信息。

话虽如此,如果市场上继续充斥着虚假或不真实的评论,那么情况显然将不再如此。评论助长了亚马逊的销售,如果人们不再信任评论,亚马逊迟早会翻车。

亚马逊一直有买家评论政策,但近年来它确实加强了监管。这是您需要知道的。

1. 不再允许奖励

亚马逊在2016年禁止了激励性评论,这种做法如今是最严重的违法行为之一。作为亚马逊卖家,您不能提供任何形式的财务奖励、折扣、免费产品或补偿,以换取对您的产品或竞争对手的评论。这包括使用第三方服务、网站和销售买家评论的社交媒体群组。

2. 您不能评论自己的产品

亚马逊的买家产品评论政策明确规定,禁止您评论自己的产品或竞争对手的产品,即使是从您自己的个人买家账户。您的家人和/或员工也要避免这样做。

3. 从不要求正面评论

虽然您可以要求买家评论您的产品,但您不能明确要求进行正面评论。许多卖家试图规避规则,将这类请求插入产品插页,但亚马逊很快抓住了这一点,并予以打击。

4. 从不要求某人更改或删除评论

一些卖家试图通过要求买家更改或删除他们的负面评论来换取补偿,这是严格禁止的。买家可以选择自行编辑或删除评论,但卖家不能影响其决定。如果评论与亚马逊社区指南相冲突,亚马逊将删除评论,所以如果您看到这种情况,请举报。

版 权 声 明

为了方便学校课堂教学,促进知识传播,便于读者学习优秀作品,本书编写过程中参考了一些网站的相关资料。为了尊重这些资料所有者的权利,特此声明,凡本书中涉及的著作权等权益,均属于原作品著作权人等。

为了维护原作品相关权益人的权益,现对本书中选用的主要作品和出处给予说明(排名不分先后)。

序号	文章	著作权归属
1	How to Become an Amazon Seller-Step by Step Guide	Bilal Uddin(Within The Flow)
2	How to Use Amazon's Shipping Template and Customize Shipping Settings for All Your Products	Seth Kniep(Just One Dime)
3	Amazon FBA Advantages and Disadvantages!	Supply Chain Game Changer
4	How To Ship To Amazon FBA-Send To Amazon Workflow(2023)	Ben Donovan(Brand Builder University)
5	A Comprehensive Guide to Perfect Amazon Product Listing Optimization	Jake Schwarzbaum(Velocity Sellers)
6	How to Write Amazon Product Titles That Drive Clicks	Armando Roggio(Practical Ecommerce)
7	9 Tips on Writing Amazon Product Descriptions	Nina Tomaro(ClearVoice)
8	Step by step guide to creating an Amazon promotion	Salesbacker
9	Amazon Advertising: How to create sponsored product automatic campaigns	Ecomclips
10	The Seller's Guide To Amazon Buyer-Seller Messages	AMZ Advisers
11	Understanding Amazon Return Policy for Amazon Sellers in 2023	FBA Masterclass
12	AMAZON FEEDBACK AND REVIEWS: WHY THEY MATTER & HOW TO GET THEM?	LandingCube

由于篇幅所限,以上列表中可能并未全部列出本书所选用的作品。在此,本书创作团队衷心感谢所有原作品的相关版权权益人及所属公司对职业教育的大力支持。由于客观原因,我们无法联系到您。如您能与我们取得联系,我们将在第一时间更正任何错误或疏漏。

与本书配套的数字资源使用说明

　　本书部分课程及与纸质教材配套数字资源以二维码链接的形式呈现。利用手机微信扫码成功后提示微信登录,授权后进入注册页面,填写注册信息。按照提示输入手机号码,点击获取手机验证码,稍等片刻收到4位数的验证码短信,在提示位置输入验证码成功,再设置密码,选择相应专业,点击"立即注册",注册成功。(若手机已经注册,则在"注册"页面底部选择"已有账号?立即注册",进入"账号绑定"页面,直接输入手机号和密码登录。)接着提示输入学习码,需刮开教材封面防伪涂层,输入13位学习码(正版图书拥有的一次性使用学习码),输入正确后提示绑定成功,即可查看二维码数字资源。手机第一次登录查看资源成功以后,再次使用二维码资源时,只需在微信端扫码即可登录进入查看。